This book is due for return not later than the
last date stamped below, unless recalled sooner.

AUSTRALIA

LBC Information Services
Sydney

CANADA and USA

Carswell
Toronto

NEW ZEALAND

Brooker's
Auckland

SINGAPORE AND MALAYSIA

Thomson Information (S.E. Asia)
Singapore

INTELLECTUAL PROPERTY IN EUROPE

SECOND SUPPLEMENT

by

GUY TRITTON
Barrister at Law

LONDON
SWEET & MAXWELL
1999

Published in 1999 by
Sweet & Maxwell Limited of
100 Avenue Road, Swiss Cottage, London NW3 3PF
(http://www.smlawpub.co.uk)
Computerset by Interactive Sciences Ltd, Gloucester
Printed and bound in Great Britain by
Headway Press, Reading

No natural forests were destroyed to make this product:
only farmed timber was used and replanted

A CIP catalogue record for this book is available from the
British Library

ISBN 0 421 61560 5

SUPPLEMENT

Introduction to Second Supplement

This supplement is the second cumulative supplement to *Intellectual Property In Europe*. Readers may be pleased to note that it is intended to publish a second edition of *Intellectual Property in Europe* in the year 2000 (hopefully by then bug-free!).

There have been a number of important developments since the book was published. First, all Member States signed the Treaty of Amsterdam on October 2, 1997. This has yet to be ratified by domestic legislative procedure for it to become law but it is anticipated that this will occur soon. The aims of the draft Treaty were ambitious and only partially realised. As such, the Amsterdam Treaty should be seen not as a Treaty in its own rights but as a successor to the Maastricht Treaty in the development of the Treaties establishing the European Union. For the purposes of this book, it does little. However, it does rather annoyingly renumber many of the Articles. The most important of these are that in the Treaty Establishing the European Community (Title II of the Maastricht Treaty) Article 30 becomes Article 28; Article 36 becomes Article 30; Articles 85 and 86 become Article 81 and 82; Article 173 becomes Article 230; Article 175 becomes Article 232; Article 177 becomes Article 234; Article 189 becomes Article 249; Article 222 becomes Article 295 and Article 235 becomes Article 308. Another important development is that the principles of subsidiarity and proportionality have been reinforced by a Protocol which is intended to define precisely the criteria for the application of these principles including the strict observance and consistent implementation by all Community institutions. Finally, there have been changes to the legislative process including the consultation and co-operation procedure that Council, Commission and Parliament must use for the purpose of enacting legislation.

In the patent field, much progress has been made with a new draft Biotechnological Directive. After the rejection of the previous draft by the European Parliament, a new draft which seeks to allay the fears of the Parliament has met with general approval. It makes clear that certain patents like for cloning human beings will be rejected under the *ordre publique* provisions. The Commission has sought to resuscitate the prospect of having a Community Patent regime by publishing a consultative document about the future of Community patents. There have also been a number of cases now about the effect of the Supplementary Protection Certificate scheme including the rejection by the European Court of Justice of a submission by Spain that it is *ultra vires*.

In the field of trade marks, the Community Trade Mark is proving a runaway success with applications three times that expected. However, oppositions are very high and there is a danger that the CTMO will become a victim of its own success as it has clearly been overwhelmed and does not have the staff. However, Alexander von Mühlendahl, the President of the CTMO has promised more staff for it. The Madrid Protocol is now in force as three months have expired since four countries ratified it. In relation to the Trade Mark Directive, there have now been a number of important cases decided by the ECJ on its provisions, in particular *Sabel* on the meaning of "likelihood of association" and *Silhouette* which renders void any domestic law provision that permitted a doctrine of international exhaustion of trade marks. Finally, there have been a number of cases with regard to the regulations protecting geographical indications of origin.

In the field of copyright, there has been one major development and that is that the Database Directive has now been adopted. The United Kingdom has now implemented it by way of statutory instrument. The deadline for its implementation has passed and a number of countries are currently subject to the threat of Commission proceedings for their failure to implement it. The final directive is much changed from the draft commented on in the book and the reader is referred to the relevant provisions set out in this supplement. The Commission has also proposed a directive dealing with the difficulties of protection in an "on line" era.

In the field of design, a deadlock arose over the "right to repair" clause that looked likely to threaten the design directive (and thus the Community Design). However, this appears now finally broken after a late night marathon session on July 24, 1998 under the conciliation procedure with a "standstill plus" clause being agreed on. This was the major point of contention and it is likely that Parliament will agree to the new draft (having participated in the conciliation procedure).

In the interaction of Article 30 to 36 and intellectual property, the ECJ in *Merck v. Primecrown* has upheld the paramount importance of consent to marketing by not overturning the case of *Merck v. Stephar* (which it was invited to reconsider) so that a person will be deemed to have exhausted any patent rights it has in a product that it puts into circulation in the Community even where the product was put in a country where no patent was available for the product. The ECJ has also confirmed its approach to parallel importers repackaging trade marked products in *Bristol-Myers Squibb v. Paranova*. Furthermore, the ECJ has confirmed in *Silhouette* that the doctrine of international exhaustion no longer applies to trade marks.

In the field of licensing, the Technology Transfer Block Exemption is in force and has simplified advisors' work when considering know-how/ patent licences and their compatibility with Article 85. In the field of franchising, the Commission has introduced a Green Paper on Vertical

Restraints which proposes taking a "rule of reason" tolerant approach to the anti-competitive effect of vertical restraints.

In the area of enforcement of EEA and E.C. competition law, there have been a number of developments including the development of "Community interest" in deciding whether the Commission must act upon a complaint. Furthermore, there have been a number of decisions and notices upon the relationship between national courts and the Commission when deciding issues arising under Community competition provisions (in particular where exemption has been or is going to be sought under Article 85(3)) and in the distribution of workload between national competition authorities and the Commission in the enforcement of Community law provisions. The Amsterdam treaty reinforces the issues of subsidiarity and this area will no doubt increase in importance.

Finally, there have been a number of important developments in the interpretation of the Brussels and Lugano Conventions on jurisdiction. In a number of English and Dutch decisions, the courts have examined the jurisdictional basis for courts issuing extraterritorial injunctions (both final and interim); what a court should do when the issue of validity of a foreign patent is raised in infringement proceedings brought in a state other than the state where the patent has been registered; the ability of patentees to sue in one country a number of infringers of parallel patents under Article 6(1) (the co-defendant rule) and the power of a court not first seized to stay proceedings where a multiplicity of proceedings have been brought in different countries relating to the infringement and validity of parallel patents. Suffice to say that Dutch and English courts have taken differing stances but the English Court of Appeal has referred in *Fort Dodge* a number of questions to the ECJ which should resolve these issues. The double actionability rule has now been abolished by the Private International Law (Miscellaneous Provisions) Act 1995.

I have endeavoured to state the law as of July 31, 1998.

Guy Tritton
One Raymond Buildings
Grays Inn

TABLE OF CONTENTS

CHAPTER ONE

INTRODUCTION

CHAPTER TWO

PATENTS IN EUROPE

CHAPTER SEVEN

ENFORCEMENT OF INTELLECTUAL PROPERTY

CHAPTER EIGHT

LICENSING OF INTELLECTUAL PROPERTY

CHAPTER NINE

INTELLECTUAL PROPERTY AND JOINT VENTURES

CHAPTER TEN

FRANCHISING

CHAPTER ELEVEN

ABUSE OF A DOMINANT POSITION

CHAPTER TWELVE

ENFORCEMENT OF E.C. AND EEA COMPETITION LAW

CHAPTER THIRTEEN

JURISDICTION AND INTELLECTUAL PROPERTY

TABLE OF CASES

(References are to paragraph numbers)

TABLE OF STATUTES

(References are to paragraph numbers)

TABLE OF STATUTORY INSTRUMENTS

(References are to paragraph numbers)

TABLE OF TREATIES AND CONVENTIONS

(References are to paragraph numbers)

TABLE OF E.C. DIRECTIVES

(References are to paragraph numbers)

TABLE OF E.C. REGULATIONS

(References are to paragraph numbers)

Chapter One

INTRODUCTION

2. European Community

(a) History of E.C. Treaty

The Treaty on European Union (TEU) has again been amended by the 1.003
Treaty of Amsterdam. This was signed on October 2, 1997. It has to be
ratified by the Member States to become law. Its aims were lofty but only
partially achieved. It should be seen as a successor to the Maastricht
Treaty. The main areas which it affects are: fundamental rights—the TEU
has now incorporated fundamental principles of liberty, democracy,
respect for human rights and other fundamental freedoms and the rule of
law; free movement of persons; non-discrimination; social policy,
employment, environment, common foreign policy, subsidiarity and proportionality. Furthermore, there has been an extension of the role of
qualified majority voting.

From the intellectual property practitioner's viewpoint, the important
changes are the reinforcement of the principle of subsidiarity and rather
annoyingly, the renumbering of the Articles in the European Community
Treaty (which forms Title II of TEU). Article 30 becomes Article 28;
Article 36 becomes Article 30; Articles 85 and 86 become Articles 81 and
82; Article 173 becomes Article 230; Article 175 becomes Article 232;
Article 177 becomes Article 234; Article 189 becomes Article 249; Arti-
cle 222 becomes Article 295 and Article 235 becomes Article 308.

(c) Source of E.C. law

(ii) Direct effect

(1) Requirements for Community provision to be "directly effective"

FOOTNOTE 26: Add: C–246/94, *Cooperative Agricola Zootecnica S* 1.012
Antonio v. Amministrazione delle Finanze dello State ECJ, September 17,
1996, unreported where the Court held that the provision was not
"unconditional" where the obligation was not qualified by any condition
or subject to the taking of any measure by the Community or by the
Member State. For the term to comply with condition (a), the Court said
that it must set out an obligation in "unequivocal terms".

(c) Directives

1.015 For a recent decision on whether or not a directive is directly effective, see C–246/94, *Cooperative della Amministrazione delle Finanze dello State* ECJ, September 17, 1996, discussed above.

(iii) Liability of Member State in damages for failure to properly implement directive

1.018 Recently, there has been some speculation in the intellectual property field about the direct applicability of TRIPS which forms part of the WTO Agreement. In *Lenzing AG's European Patent (UK)* [1997] R.P.C. 245, it was held in the English High Court that it was *acte claire* that TRIPS was not susceptible to being directly invoked in Community or Member States' courts. The main reason for this is that the WTO Agreement contains an express provision that it is not capable of being directly invoked in such courts and that its predecessor GATT had been held not to be directly applicable in Cases 21–24/72 *International Fruit Co N.V. v. Produktschap voor Groenten en Fruit* [1972] E.C.R. 1219; [1975] 2 C.M.L.R. 1. See also *Judicial Review of the EPO and the Direct Effect of TRIPS in the European Community* [1997] EIPR 367.

1.022 In Joined Cases C–46/93, *Brasserie du Pecheur v. Germany* and C–48/93, *R. v. Secretary of State for Transport ex p. Factortame Ltd and Others*, Judgment of ECJ, March 5, 1996 [1996] 1 C.M.L.R. 889, the Court of Justice has ruled that Member States of the European Union are liable to compensate individuals for damage caused by serious infringements of directly effective provisions of Community law. A German and English case were referred to the ECJ under Article 177. In both cases, national legislation had previously been held by the ECJ to infringe Community law (see Case 178/84, *E.C. Commission v. Germany* [1987] E.C.R. 1227 [1988] 1 C.M.L.R. 780 and C–221/89, *Factortame (No. 3)* [1991] I E.C.R. 3905, 3 C.M.L.R. 589).

The Court held that the principle of State liability for damage caused to individuals by infringements of Community law had been established in *Francovich v. Italy*. The Court held that a right to reparation arose where the rule of Community law infringed was intended to confer rights on individuals; the breach was sufficiently serious and the breach directly caused damage to individuals. In determining whether the breach was sufficiently serious, the decisive test was whether the Member State manifestly and gravely disregarded the limits on its discretion. The Court gave guidance on the factors which the national courts should consider with respect to this condition. The factors included the clarity and precision of the rule breached, the measure of discretion left to the national authorities, whether the infringement and damage caused were intentional or involuntary, whether any error of law was excusable and whether the position taken by Community institutions may have contributed towards the Member State's breach of Community law. It held that a breach of Community law will clearly be sufficiently serious if it has persisted despite a judgment finding the infringement to be established or in the light of settled case law. It is a matter for the national court to decide whether a breach is sufficiently serious to justify the imposition of liability in damages. As regards the last condition, the national court must assess whether there was a direct causal link between the breach of the obligation borne by the State and the damage sustained by the applicant.

In considering the extent of reparation, the Court stated that it must be commensurate with the loss sustained, so as to ensure the effective protection of Community law rights. Provisions governing claims for compensation should not be less favourable than those applying to similar domestic claims and they should include the right to exemplary damages for unconstitutional or oppressive conduct where this is provided for in national law for like claims.

Generally, a failure to implement a directive within the allocated time period will constitute a manifest and serious breach and consequently gives rise to a right of reparation for individuals if the result prescribed by the directive entails the grant to individuals of rights whose content is identifiable and a causal link exists between the breach of the State's obligation and the loss and damage suffered—*Dillenkofer and ors v. Germany* [1996] 3 C.M.L.R. 469 (ECJ).

(e) Enforcement of Community law

(i) Preliminary rulings procedure of ECJ

In *Phytheron International S.A. v Jean Bourdon SA* C–352/95 [1997]   **1.026**
F.S.R. 937, the Court of Justice emphasised that it could only answer the national's courts question on the basis of the facts as they appeared from the order for reference. In particular, in the context of proceedings raising an important point on the extent of a trade mark owner's rights, the Court should not depart from the stated facts because the owner of the mark, not being a party to the main proceedings, could not put its argument to the Court.

A procedural rule in a Member State that prevents a national court   **1.027**
from considering of its own motion whether or not a measure of domestic law is compatible with a provision of Community law will normally be contrary to Community law—see C–312/93, *Peterbroeck v. Van Campenhout & Cie* [1996] 1 C.M.L.R. 793. See also similar case in C–430 & 431/93, *Van Schijndel v. Stichting Pensioenfonds voor Fysiotherapeuten* [1996] 1 C.M.L.R. 801.

The Court of Justice has given a useful guidance to national courts in relation to references under Article 177 based on its case law—*Guidance on references by national courts for preliminary rulings* [1997] 1 C.M.L.R. 78. This can be summarised as follows:

3

(a) Courts or tribunals against whose decisions there is no judicial remedy under national law must refer questions of interpretation arising before them unless the Court has already ruled on the point or unless the correct application of the rule of Community law is obvious.

(b) Where a national court intends to question the validity of a Community act, it must refer that question to the Court of Justice but may reject a plea challenging the validity of such an act.

(c) Where the national court has serious doubts about the validity of a Community act, it may grant interim or suspensory relief.

(d) The order for reference should contain a statement of reasons which is succinct but sufficiently complete to give the Court, and those to whom it must be notified, a clear understanding of the factual and legal context of the proceedings. In particular, it should include.

> (i) a statement of the facts which are essential to a full understanding of the legal significance of the main proceedings
> (ii) an exposition of the national law which may be applicable
> (iii) a statement of the reasons which have prompted the national court to refer the question or questions to the Court of Justice and
> (iv) where appropriate, a summary of the arguments of the parties

(e) It is desirable that a decision to refer should not be taken until the national court is able to define, if only as a working hypothesis, the factual and legal context of the question; such is best done after both sides have been heard.

(ii) Judicial review of acts of Community institutions

1.028   In T–116/94R, *Cassa Nazionale di Previdenza ed Assistenza a favore degli Avvocati e Procuratori v. E.U. Council* [1996] 2 C.M.L.R. 79, the CFI held that a regulation is not of direct and individual concern to an applicant who applies for annulment of the regulation under Article 173 where the applicant is affected by the regulation by virtue of belonging to a class defined in general and abstract terms. See also T–472/93, *Campo Ebro Industrial S.A. v. E.U. Council* [1996] 1 C.M.L.R. 1038.

(f) E.C. and intellectual property

1.034A   In a recent case, the validity of *Community substantive* intellectual property legislation has been considered. In *Spain v. E.U. Council* [1996]

1 C.M.L.R. 415 (ECJ), the ECJ was concerned with the validity of the E.C. Regulation which permitted patentees of pharmaceutical drugs to apply for a Supplemental Protection Certificate where there had been a delay in the grant of marketing authorisation for the drug (generally see para 2.115 *et seq* of the book). If the certificate is granted, this effectively extends the life of the patent via the certificate process. Spain and Greece argued that in the allocation of powers between the Community and Member States, Articles 36 and 222 of the E.C. Treaty meant that Member States had exclusive sovereignty over industrial property matters and that the Community had no power to regulate substantive patent law and could only harmonise those aspects relating to the exercise of industrial property rights which are capable of having an effect upon the achievement of the general objectives laid down in the Treaty. They submitted that such action could not take the form of a new industrial property right in particular that which in effect changed the duration of a patent.

This argument raised an important issue about the jurisdiction of the Community to legislate for *substantive* intellectual property rights as opposed to merely restricting the rights of intellectual property rights owner to exercise such rights. The Court rejected the argument that Articles 36 and 222 reserve exclusively to Member States the ability to enact new i.p.r. Moreover, the Court said that the effect of Article 235 and Articles 100 and 100a was to confer competence on the Community to harmonise national laws in the field of intellectual property (referring to Opinion 1/94 [1994] I E.C.R. 5267, para 59). Such provisions entitled the Community, in order to achieve the objectives of the Treaty to legislate in the field of intellectual property, in particular the attainment of an internal market without frontiers (Article 7a).

The Court held that the adoption of a regulation conferring a supplemental protection certificate was aimed at harmonising differing national laws on the grant of supplemental protection certificate. Thus, when it was adopted, two Member States had enacted for such a right and another state was preparing to do so. By providing for a community wide right, the regulation was aimed at preventing the fragmentation of the internal market whereby the medicine would be protected in some states but not others. Accordingly, the Court rejected the further argument by Spain and Greece that there was no legal basis under Articles 100a and 235 for enacting the SPC Regulation.

N.B. Article 7a of the E.C. Treaty provides that the Community shall adopt measures with the "aim of progressively establishing the internal market" over a period expiring on December 31, 1992 in accordance with *inter alia* Article 100a. The internal market is defined as comprising "an area without internal frontiers in which the free movement of goods, persons, services and capital is ensured in accordance with the provisions of this Treaty."

Article 100a confers power on the E.U. Council to adopt legislative measures which have as their object the establishment and functioning of an internal market by way of a qualified majority.

Article 222 states "This Treaty shall in no way prejudice the rules in Member States governing the system of property ownership".

Article 235 states that "If action by the Community should prove necessary to attain, in the course of the operation of the common market, one of the objectives of the Community and this Treaty has not provided the necessary powers, the Council, shall acting unanimously on a proposal from the Commission and after consulting the European Parliament, take the appropriate measures".

Chapter Two

PATENTS IN EUROPE

3. Patent Co-operation Treaty

(j) Table of European Contracting States of PCT

Bosnia-Herzegovina has acceded to PCT.   2.022

4. European Patent Convention

(a) Fundamentals of EPC

(i) Scheme of the EPC

Add: The creation of a basket of national patents following the grant of   2.024
a European patent gives rise to jurisdictional problems if the European
patent is subject to opposition proceedings because national courts of the
designated states may be seized of patent infringement proceedings and
indeed revocation proceedings whilst the future of the European patent
in toto is still in doubt. This occurred in *Beloit Technologies v. Valmet
Paper Machinery Inc* [1997] R.P.C. 489 (Court of Appeal, England)
where proceedings for infringement and a counterclaim of invalidity of
an English patent granted pursuant to the grant of a European patent
were being tried at the same time as appeals from oppositions in the EPO
were being pursued (and the possibility of the patents being amended in
such appeals). The Court of Appeal held that s.77(2) of the Patents Act
1977 (which states that the provisions of the Patent Act do not affect the
operation of any provisions of the EPC) did not remove the right of the
UK courts to revoke an invalid European patent (UK) at any time after
grant even if there were current opposition proceedings in which the
patentee was reserving its position about amending the patent. The
patentee had the right to amend the patent in the UK proceedings. Thus,
the court (upheld on appeal) revoked the EP(UK) patent. The Court of
Appeal held that the Patents Court should only stay proceedings in
England pending a final resolution of EPO proceedings if the latter could
be resolved quickly and a stay would not inflict injustice on a party or be
against the public interest. Normally, this is not the case because opposition proceedings can be very long.

See also *Petrolite Holdings Inc v. Dyno-Oil Field Chemicals U.K. Ltd*
[1998] F.S.R. 190 where the Patents Court held that a European Patent

(U.K.) be revoked unless the plaintiffs applied to amend in the United Kingdom despite the plaintiff's proposal to amend the patent in suit before the Opposition Division of the EPO.

(ii) EPC and harmonisation of national patent laws

2.026 FOOTNOTE 50: Add: In Adams, "Choice of Forum in Patent Disputes" [1995] EIPR 497, he compares patent litigation in England and Wales, Scotland, France and Germany. He notes that construction of claims in the first two are traditionally narrow, in France somewhat broader and Germany has the broadest construction of claims.

(b) Substantive requirements for a European patent
(i) Novelty

2.033 *Availability to the public*—FOOTNOTE 82: Add: However, see T–455/91, *GENENTECH/Expression in yeast* [1996] EPOR 87 where it was held that an oral disclosure at an International Conference by a lecturer which included an advance abstract, a subsequent paper, a poster presentation and workshop discussions constituted prior art for the purpose of novelty.

A factory-scale experiment conducted by the patentee around six months prior to the priority date in the opponent's works on account of the patentee's lack of available facilities for large-scale experiments was held to be an enabling disclosure which invalidated the patent as the parties were not subject to a tacit or express duty to maintain secrecy—T–602/91 *BAYER/Plasterboard* [1996] EPOR 388.

In T–385/92 *UNILEVER/Deodorant Detergent* [1996] EPOR 579, the TBA held that a premature disclosure of an application of the closest prior art document by the Brazilian Patent Office was not an evident abuse which would prevent it being treated as prior art, despite the detriment suffered by the patentee as a result because there existed no relationship between the patentee and the Brazilian Patent Office and the disclosure was a mere error.

2.034 *Enabling disclosure*—In T–793/93, *ALLIED SIGNAL/Polyolefin fiber* [1996] EPOR 104, the TBA was concerned with whether certain prior art documents anticipated the claimed invention. The opponent claimed that the inevitable outcome of an express literal disclosure of certain documents was the anticipation of the claimed invention. The TBA said that the term "available to the public" clearly goes beyond literal or diagrammatic description and implies a communication express or implicit of technical information by other means as well. In the case where a prior art document fails explicitly to disclose something falling within a claim, availability in the sense of Article 54 may still be established if the inevitable outcome of what is literally or explicitly disclosed falls within the ambit of that claim (at 109). The Opponent accepted that there was a measure of uncertainty as to the outcome of the prior art documents but submitted that on the balance of probability, it was more likely than not that the disclosure of the documents would inevitably lead to something falling within the claims in suit. The TBA rejected this approach and held that in deciding what is or is not the inevitable outcome of an express literal disclosure in a particular prior art document, a standard of proof of "beyond all reasonable doubt" needs to be applied. If any such doubt existed as to what might or might not be the result of carrying out the literal disclosure and instructions of a prior art, then the case on anticipation failed.

(ii) Inventive Step

Objective approach—In an interesting case, T–465/92, *ALCAN/ Aluminium alloys* [1995] EPOR 501, the TBA revisited the "problem and solution" approach. It pointed out that its weakness is that it relies on the results of a search of the relevant prior art which is made with actual knowledge of the invention and is thus inherently based on hindsight and thus requires care in its application. Furthermore, the TBA pointed out that it can result in complicated multi-step reasoning where the facts are clear, either for or against inventiveness. Accordingly, the TBA said "if an invention breaks entirely new ground, it may suffice to say that there is no close prior art, rather than constructing a problem based on what is tenuously regarded as the closest prior art" (at para. 9.5). The TBA went on to say that it saw a welcome trend in recent unreported decisions which have emphasised that the investigation of inventiveness should avoid formulating artificial and unrealistic technical problems and should normally start from the technical problems identified in the patent in suit (at para. 9.6). See also T–495/91, *PENGULAN/Surface finish* [1995] EPOR 516 and T–741/91, *UENO/BON–3–acid* [1995] EPOR 533.   2.037

FOOTNOTE 7: Add "See also T141/87 *BOSCH/Diagnostic test system for motor vehicles* [1996] EPOR 570 where the TBA held that claim 1 of the patent was not inventive because it could be solved by a team consisting of a housing specialist and a plugged connections specialist and there was no synergistic effect arising from the interaction of the three claimed features in Claim 1.   2.038

Ex post facto analysis—Where a problem was capable of being solved by combining two prior art documents, the invention will still be held inventive if the possibility of thereby solving the problem would only have been readily apparent from ex post facto analysis T–323/90, *PHILIP MORRIS/Tobacco lamina filler* [1996] EPOR 422.   2.040

2.045A Insert as new paragraph:

Disadvantages of prior art — In an interesting case, T–1027/93, *L'AIR LIQUIDE/Gas separation* [1996] EPOR 188, the claim was for the separation of gas mixtures by means of a semipermeable membrane whereby the inventive part was balancing the partial pressure of one of the gas components on both sides of the membrane so that there was no partial pressure differential over the membrane. The Opposition Division rejected the patent because it noted that there was a much better way of achieving the same effect, namely adding sufficient concentrations of another gas to the feed side. However, the Technical Board of Appeal held that the mere fact that there might be a much more effective way of carrying out the same task did not render the claim unpatentable. Indeed, it said that "the apparent futility of achieving this by carrying out the claimed process cannot be said to be obvious. In fact in view of this futility, it could be said to be completely non-obvious." Accordingly, a patent for an invention which is clearly unwieldy and where there is a more obvious route will, because of such points, often be patentable!

2.045B *Unexpected side effect* — In T–386/89 *GKN SANKEY/Tractor Wheels* [1996] EPOR 37, the Technical Board of Appeal held that where the solution of the problem set out in the patent application was obvious, the patent was not saved by an unexpected side effect (applying T–21/81 *ALLEN-BRADLEY/ Electromagnetically operated switch* [1979–1985] EPOR Vol. B 342). Furthermore, where the patent specification does not disclose the unexpected side effect or indeed state the problem which is solved by the unexpected side effect, then if such is not deducible from the application as originally filed, it cannot be taken into account when assessing the problem underlying the invention for the purpose of assessing the issue of inventive step.

2.045C *Old Prior Art* — The mere fact that there is a long period between the prior art and the invention does not *per se* demonstrate inventiveness but may assist if the patentee is able to prove that during that time there had existed an unsatisfied requirement that the invention solved — T–324/94 *VDO ADOLF SCHINDLING/Illuminating Device* [1997] EPOR 146. See also T–964/92 *EISAI/Benzodioxane derivatives* [1997] EPOR 201 where it was held that the age of a cited document is a pointer to the presence of inventive step but is only a subsidiary pointer where obviousness does not already follow from other reasons.

2.045D *Inventive step in biotechnology inventions* — In T–923/92 *GENENTECH/t-PA* [1996] EPOR 275, the invention was for a process which comprised the preparation of a protein which had a particular amino acid sequence. In effect, Genentech had found a method for cloning and expressing human t-PA in a recombinant host. The appellants argued that there was considerable interest in arriving at a solution to this problem and that the skilled person would have arrived at a solution by following the prior art. On the other hand, the patentees argued that all the uncertainties and problems that the skilled person had to face (low abundance of mRNA, size of mRNA, unknown amino acid sequence of human t-PA and so on) showed that the solution to the problem was far from straightforward. The Technical Board of Appeal found that although there was much incentive for solving the problem as the patentees had, the task was regarded as tough, the prospects of success were considered thin, and the announcement of the isolation by the patentees of a full-length clone encoding human t-PA was received in the interested milieux as a pleasant surprise. Accordingly, the Board concluded that there was an inventive step (N.B. national patents based on the same invention (although the claims were cast differently) were held invalid in England—see *GENENTECH/t-PA* [1987] R.P.C 553 upheld on appeal [1989] R.P.C 147).

(v) Categories of inventions deemed unpatentable

See T–1002/92, *PETTERSSON/Queueing system* [1996] EPOR 1, whereby a party failed to prove that the patent claimed for was a method for doing business.   2.048

After second paragraph, add: In *HOWARD FLOREY/Relaxin* (App. No. 83 307 553) [1995] EPOR 541, Opposition was brought by the Green Party of the European Parliament to the grant of a patent for H2–relaxin which had had no previously recognised existence. The patentee had developed a process for obtaining H2–relaxin and the DNA encoding it, had characterised these products by their chemical structure and had found a use of the protein. A typical claim was for a DNA fragment with a certain amino acid sequence. The Green Party claimed that the subject matter of the opposed patent lacked novelty and were mere discoveries since the gene that encodes relaxin has always been present in the female human body. The Opposition Division rejected this ground stating that the claims to cDNAs (*i.e.* DNA copies of human mRNA encoding relaxin) did not occur in the human body. However, it went on to consider the position where the claims consisted of claims to natural DNA fragments encoding H2–relaxin and the latter had not been known before and had no previously recognised existence. It said that it was established patent practice to recognise novelty for a natural substance which had been isolated for the first time and had no previously recognised existence (see Guidelines C-IV 2.3).

Footnote 38: Add "The reference to Beattie is *BEATTIE/Marker* [1992] EPOR 221. See also T–77/92 *BROSELOW/Measuring tape* [1998] EPOR 266 where the TBA upheld an appeal against the decision of the Examining Division that the invention was not patentable because it did not include any new technical feature over and above the prior art.

(1) Computer-related inventions

2.050   See also T–769/92, *SOHEI/General purpose management system* [1996] EPOR 253 where a claim for a computer system for plural types of independent management, including financial and inventory management whereby data can be input via a single transfer slip appearing on the VDU and then processed for all of the types of management, was held patentable as the transfer slip was a user interface involving technical considerations and not merely the presentation of information or computer programming as such. See "The Patentability of Computer-Related Inventions in Europe" *Newman* [1997] 12 EIPR 701.

(2) Biotechnological inventions

2.051   Where it is claimed that the biotechnological invention is merely a claim for a naturally occurring substance and thus is a discovery, see *HOWARD FLOREY/Relaxin* discussed at para. 2.048 and below.

2.052   *Animal inventions*—At end of paragraph, add: In *HOWARD FLOREY/Relaxin* (App. No. 83 307 553) [1995] EPOR 541, the Green Party in opposition proceedings claimed that a patent for a DNA fragment encoding human H2–relaxin (discussed above at 2.048) offended against the provisions of Article 53(a). Their arguments were that it was immoral to take the gene from tissue of a pregnant woman, it was a form of modern slavery because it involved the dismemberment of women and their piecemeal sale to commercial enterprises, and the patenting of human genes meant that human life was being patented and this was immoral. In an interesting judgment, the Opposition Division rejected all these arguments. However, many of these arguments have now been taken up by the European Parliament in relation to the draft biotechnological directive and have been implemented. See para 2.114

2.053   *Plant inventions*—T–356/93 *PLANT GENETIC SYSTEMS/Glutamine synthetase inhibitors (Opposition by Greenpeace)* is reported at [1995] EPOR 357 (the official name for *Plant Genetic Sciences and Biogen*). For discussion of this case, see Llewelyn, "Greenpeace v. Plant Genetic Systems NV" [1995] EIPR 506 and Schrell, "Are Plants Still Patentable?" [1995] EIPR 242.

In G03/95 *Inadmissible referral* [1996] EPOR 505, the President of the EPO referred to the Enlarged Board of Appeal the issue as to whether the decision in *PLANT GENETIC SYSTEMS* was incompatible with the decisions in *CIBA-GEIGY/Propagating material* and *HARVARD/Oncomouse*. In particular, the question referred was whether a claim "which related to plants or animals but wherein specific plant or animal varieties are not individually claimed "contravened Article 53(b) if it embraced plant or animal varieties". The EBA declined to answer the question because in their opinion the decisions did not conflict. The EBA held that the reason that the TBA had found that Claim 21 of the *Plant Genetic Systems* was contrary to Article 53(b) was because the claimed genetic modification which formed the essence of Claim 21 was in reality a claim to a plant variety because the herbicide-resistance character imparted to the tobacco plant was distinctive and stable in succeeding generations of the plants so that it equated to the creation of a new plant variety. For all intents and purposes, the invention was a claim to a plant variety *per se*. Thus, the EBA held that the TBA in *Plant Genetic Systems* did not reject the claim on the basis that it *embraced* known plant varieties but because it was upon proper analysis for a plant variety.

(3) Methods and products for medical and veterinary treatment

FOOTNOTE 66: Add: See also T–82/93, *TELECTRONICS/Pacer* [1996] EPOR 409 where an invention for the method of operating a pacer in accordance with the cardiac output required whilst a person exercised was held to fall within the prohibition of Article 52(4). | 2.055

At end of first paragraph, add: In T–820/92, *GENERAL HOSPITAL/ Contraceptive method* [1995] EPOR 446, the TBA held that a claim for a method for preventing pregnancy in female mammals amounted to a method for treatment by therapy within the meaning of Article 52(4). However, it permitted claims for "the use of a composition, an oestrogenic steroid and a progestational steroid in the preparation of an agent for preventing pregnancy" (so-called "Swiss style" claims) on the basis of G–05/93, *EISAI*.

(4) Claims for non-medical uses of a known product

Where a new technical feature is claimed from a known process, *Mobil Oil* cannot be relied on as meaning that the disclosure in the patent application of a new technical effect which was not described before should necessarily be considered as also involving an inventive step—see T–329/99, *FUJITSU/Silicon oxynitride semiconductor* [1996] EPOR 224. | 2.058

(vi) Selection inventions

In *AGREVO/Triazole sulphonamides* [1996] EPOR 171, the Technical Board of Appeal considered a patent for a group of triazole sulphonamides possessing herbicidal activity and claimed as chemical compounds *per se*. The claims were wide, including claims to a multitude of "substituted" triazole sulphonamides. The Examining Division rejected the claim inter alia on the basis that having regard to the fact that the technical effect claimed was herbicidal, "substituted" could not be given its ordinary technical meaning of substituted by absolutely anything. On appeal, the TBA considered a number of issues relating to claims for a | 2.059

broad category of chemical compounds. The TBA said that a selection of compounds in order to be patentable must not be arbitrary but must be justified by a hitherto unknown technical effect which is caused by those structural features which distinguish the claimed compounds from the numerous other compounds.

The assessment of the technical contribution to the art must take account of the actual technical reason for providing the claimed compounds as distinct from the host of other theoretically possible modified chemical compounds. If a number of compounds claimed is such that it is inherently unlikely that all of them, or at least substantially all of them, will possess the promised activity, then the burden of proof of the possession of that activity rests on the shoulders of the person asserting it. In the case, the applicant's test results provided in the description for some of the claimed compounds were inadequate to lead to the inference that substantially all the claimed compounds possessed the desired herbicidal activity. Accordingly, the claim failed.

FOOTNOTE 89: Add: See also T–247/91, *STAMICARBON/Cyclohexane oxidation* [1996] EPOR 120 where a claim for a process for making cyclohexanol using a temperature range of 85–115°C as being novel over the prior art which disclosed the same process but over a broader range of 80–170°C because of the surprising effect that in the subrange a higher yield per time unit for a lower energy input is obtained was rejected by the TBA. In particular, the TBA held that the applicant's submission that the subrange selected was novel because of the surprising effect that it had as judged against the whole range was not relevant, because a subrange selected from a larger range cannot be rendered new by virtue of a newly discovered effect but must be new per se (following Hoechst). It is submitted that the TBA's reasoning in this case is flawed because having stated the principle in *Hoechst*, they failed to decide whether the surprising effect meant that the invention was new *per se*. A surprising effect of a subrange can be novel over a disclosed broader range as indeed was the case in *Hoechst* where it was held that a selection of the use of the catalyst in the amount 0.02–0.2 mol per cent was novel in a chemical process as against the prior art which disclosed the use of catalyst in the same process in the amount 0–100 mol per cent because the selection was not arbitrary as it gave rise to a substantial improvement in yield and, moreover, it was not obvious because one would normally expect a lower concentration of catalyst to reduce the yield. If such an approach is applied to *STAMICARBON*, one would have thought that such was patentable because the subrange selected produced a surprising effect (*i.e.* a higher yield per minute at a lower energy input). Indeed, the only real fundamental difference between *Hoechst* and *STAMICARBON* is that the ratio of the subrange to the range disclosed in the former was a mere fraction of the corresponding ratio in the latter. However, in the former case, if the owner of the prior art patent selected the 0.02 to 0.2 mol ratio, it would probably only be because he wished to take advantage of the surprising effect discovered by Hoechst, whereas the owner of the prior art in *STAMICARBON* would have had to be careful not to infringe the selection patent applied for because it covered such a large range of the prior art's range.

See also T–133/92 *AKZO/Bleaching activators* [1996] EPOR 558 where the TBA held that it does not follow that if a choice of a narrower range is inventive, then there must of necessity be selective novelty in it. Thus, the TBA held that a claim for a bleaching agent wherein the claim was for a C_6–C_{12} alkyl group as against the prior art which disclosed a C_6–C_{15} alkyl group was not selectively novel because a skilled person would have considered those compounds containing lower alkyl groups as being the most preferred compounds because of their easier accessibility and their better solubility in water. However, in granting an auxiliary request, the TBA held that there is novelty where the prior art discloses a family of compounds defined by a general structural formula covering the particular compound but does not describe it explicitly.

(c) Practice and procedure under the EPC

FOOTNOTE 3: Add to end "This judgment is now fully reported as G03/92   2.062
LATCHWAYS/Unlawful applicant [1995] EPOR 141.

(v) Contents of the patent application

Claims

FOOTNOTE 52: Add: See T–454/89, *ICI/Optical sensing apparatus* [1995]   2.069
EPOR 600 for a case where the TBA held that the claims had to be clear without referring to the description. The TBA held that Article 84 requires that the claims are clear in themselves when being read with the normal skills including the knowledge about the prior art, but not including any knowledge derived from the description of the patent application or amended patent (at p. 609).

FOOTNOTE 55: Add: See also T–850/90, *HUTCHINSON/Tyre locking device* [1996] EPOR 439.

(vi) Fees

In a recent study on costs, the EPO has reported that on average   2.073
45,510DM is needed for a European patent with eight designated countries—7,800DM for the preparation of an application; 14,500DM for proceeding up to the grant of a patent and 23,310DM for the national stage. It was noted that translation costs come to one-third of total costs.

In T–575/94 *GILLS' CABLES* [1997] EPOR 100, an opponent relied   2.075
upon witness statements relating to an instance of prior use. The patentee argued that there was doubt about the credibility of the witnesses' statements and averred that there was no absolute proof. The TBA held the following:

15

"It is to be noted in this context that the EPC does not contain any provisions restricting acceptable means of proof. Neither are there particular provisions about the evaluation of evidence or about how the outcome of taking of evidence should be assessed. In accordance with the case law of the Boards of Appeal, the principle of free evaluation of evidence applies. This means that the Board must reach its decision on the basis of the whole of the evidence provided and in the light of the conclusion it reaches after careful evaluation of that evidence.

The decision need not be based on absolute proof, which, particularly where it is alleged that a prior use took place a long time ago, would amount to an unreasonable burden, but *should be based on a degree of probability, which, in human experience, verges on certainty*" [at p. 110—my emphasis].

For a case where the evidence of prior user was disregarded because of its flimsiness, see T–441 *MAELZER/Adaptor* [1997] EPOR 177. See also T–472/92 *SEKISUI/Shrinkable Sheet* [1997] EPOR 432 where it was held that the burden of proof in relation to evidence of prior use should be beyond reasonable doubt because there was unlikely to be any evidence available to the patentee to contradict it. See also T–750/94 *AT&T/Proof of prior publication* [1997] EPOR 509.

(d) Prosecution of application before EPO

(viii) Amendments

2.089   *Procedure and Practice*—After first paragraph, add: For the principles applying to the grant of leave to amend a patent during oral proceedings during opposition proceedings, see T–626/90, *TERUMO/Production of peptides* (amendments permitted) [1996] EPOR 194 and T–28/92, *PROCTER/Oral compositions* (amendments denied) [1996] EPOR 305.

2.090   *Substantive law*—In principle, an amendment by way of change of a claim from a method of operating a device to the device itself which is proposed during opposition proceedings is not allowable under Article 123(3)—see T–82/93, *TELECTRONICS/Pacer* [1996] EPOR 409. In G01/93 *Advanced Semiconductor Products/Limiting feature* [1995] EPOR 97, the EBA held that the main purpose of Article 123(2) and (3) was "to create a fair balance between the interests of applicants and the patentees, on the one hand, and competitors and other third parties on the other . . .".

Deletion of feature in claim—In T–190/83 *OTTO BOCK/Artificial knee joint* [1998] EPOR 272, the TBA held that "the content of the application" in Article 123(2) is the totality of the original disclosure and this constitutes a "reservoir" from which the applicant can draw. Thus, where an applicant sought to omit two features and add one feature to Claim 1, the omission of the features could not constitute a breach of Article 123(2) (N.B. the date of this recently reported decision is July 24, 1984 and thus must be read in the light of the *Kabushiki* and *Advanced Semiconductor Products* in relation to the addition of a feature).

FOOTNOTE 73: Add "See also T–136/88 *Van Der Lely/Soil cultivating implement* [1996] EPOR 67 where it was held that the deletion of a feature of Claim 1 during opposition proceedings was impermissible because the feature was clearly put forward as being necessary to solve the originally indicated problem and an invention without the feature was neither disclosed or appeared intended by the description. *Quaere* —The deletion of a feature in a claim invariably widens the scope of the claim and is thus surely impermissible at an opposition stage by reason of Article 123(3) which prohibits amendments at an opposition stage where such is to extend the protection conferred by the claims.

Addition of undisclosed limiting feature—In T–873/94 *KABU-SHIKI KAISHA/Divisional Application* [1998] EPOR 71, the TBA, held in applying *ADVANCED SEMICONDUCTOR PRODUCTS/Limiting feature* [1995] EPOR 97, that the addition to a claim before grant of an undisclosed limiting feature may or not constitute subject matter which extends beyond the content of the application as filed, depending on circumstances. Generally, if the added feature provides a technical contribution to the subject matter (*i.e.* contributes to the inventiveness) and is not disclosed in the application, it will be impermissible. If on the other hand, the feature in question merely excludes protection for part of the subject matter, it will be permissible. The TBA held that the novelty test may not always be appropriate in order to determine whether or not an amended application is contrary to Article 123(2).

In considering whether the added feature goes beyond providing a mere limitation but involves a technical contribution to the claimed invention, one must consider how it interacts with the other features of the claim so as to solve or assist the solution of the technical problem as it is understood by the skilled person—see T–384/91, *ADVANCED SEMICONDUCTOR PRODUCTS/Optical membrane* [1996] EPOR 125 applying G–01/93 *ADVANCED SEMICONDUCTOR PRODUCTS/Limiting feature* [1995] EPOR. 97.

Amendments in appellate proceedings for Opposition Division—On appeal, the principle of *reformatio in peius* (an appellant should not be put in a worse position than if it had not appealed) means that where a party in opposition proceedings appeals a decision by the Opposition Division to permit claims and the respondent patentee responds by seeking to amend claims (and has itself not sought to appeal the decision), the patentee cannot obtain claims which are broader in

scope than that maintained by the Opposition Division (see T–923/92 *GENENTECH/t-PA* [1996] EPOR 275).

FOOTNOTE 77: Add:

"In G–01/93 *ADVANCED SEMICONDUCTOR PRODUCTS/ Limiting feature* [1995] EPOR 97, the EBA held there is no mutual relationship between Article 123(2) and 123(3). Thus, during opposition proceedings, if a limiting feature is considered to fall under Article 123(2), it cannot be maintained in the patent in view of Article 100c nor can it be removed without widening the scope of the claims contrary to Article 123(3). The EBA noted that this could operate harshly against an applicant who amends his application during examination in response to an *ex parte* objection and then has that amendment challenged during opposition proceedings but such followed from Article 123.

2.092 Add: In the United Kingdom, the Court of Appeal has held that a UK patent granted pursuant to a European patent can be revoked notwithstanding that it is subject to opposition proceedings—*Beloit Technologies Inc v. Valmet Paper Machinery Inc* 1997 R.P.C. 443 (discussed in detail at para 2.024 above).

(xi) Appeals

2.093 On appeal, the principle of *reformatio in peius* (an appellant should not be put in a worse position than if it had not appealed) means that where a party in opposition proceedings appeals a decision by the Opposition Division to permit claims and the respondent patentee responds by seeking to amend claims (and has itself not sought to appeal the decision), the patentee cannot obtain claims which are broader in scope than that maintained by the Opposition Division (see T–923/92 *Genentech/ t-PA* [1996] EPOR 275).

In G–01/95 *THOMAS DE LA RUE/Grounds for Opposition* [1996] EPOR 601 and G–07/95 *ETHICON/Coated surgical staple* [1997] EPOR 89, the Enlarged Board of Appeal held applying G–09/91 and G–10/91 *ROHOM & HAAS/Power to examine* [1993] EPOR 485 that a fresh ground of opposition (which means a new legal basis for objecting to the maintenance of the patent which was not raised and substantiated in the notice of opposition and was not introduced into the opposition proceedings by a party or the Opposition Division) could not be raised in appellate proceedings. Thus, in appeal proceedings where only novelty and inventive step were in issue, it was not open to the TBA to consider whether the invention was a patentable discovery because it represented unpatentable subject matter based on Article 52.

In *ex parte* proceedings prior to grant, the TBA may consider grounds not considered by the Examining Board—see G–10/93 *SIEMENS/Scope of examination in ex p. appeal* [1997] EPOR 227.

FOOTNOTE 14: Add: Appeals only lie from decisions of the relevant division. Thus, where the Vice-President of Directorate-General V wrote to the appellant setting out his contentions, this did not constitute a decision as it did not emanate from the Legal Division and constituted merely a reply to a letter from the appellants' representatives—see J–02/93 *EBA/Decisions subject to appeal* [1996] EPOR 149.

In *R v. Comptroller General of Patents ex p. Lenzing* [1997] R.P.C. 245, the High Court held that a decision of the EPO Boards of Appeal was not judicially reviewable in the United Kingdom. See also *Judicial Review of the EPO and the Direct Effect of TRIPS in the European Community* [1997] EIPR 367.

Where the failure to comply with time limits has been brought about by the conduct of the EPO, it has been held that it is contrary to the principle of good faith governing relations between the EPO and the applicant and the principle of *venire contra factum proprium* and that in such exceptional circumstances, the Legal Board of Appeal deemed the late payment of a renewal fee to have been paid on time even though the period for re-establishment of rights in relation to late payment of renewal fees (one year) had expired—J–14/94 *EXPANDED METAL CO./Principle of good faith* [1996] EPOR 327.   **2.095**

In G–02/95 *ATOTECH/Correction* [1997] EPOR 77, the EBA held that EPCr 88 was subject to Article 123(2) (amendments to a European patent application may only be allowed provided that the subject matter does not extend beyond the content of the application as filed). Thus, a correction to the documents which make up the filed application (description, claims and where appropriate the drawings) may not be made if such is to breach Article 123(2). Accordingly, where an agent had mistakenly filed the description and claims of another application in a request for grant, such documents cannot be replaced by way of a correction under EPCr 88 with the documents which the agents had intended to file with their request (and as a result, the application was not able to be accorded the original filing date).   **2.097**

6. COMMUNITY PATENT MEASURES

(a) Community patent convention

In June 1997, the Commission issued a Green Paper dealing with promoting and protecting innovation in Europe through patents—*Community Patents and the patent system in Europe* COM (97) 314. It is intended to be a consultative document to determine whether users' needs are being met at a Community level. The central part of the Green Paper is devoted to the Community patent and the adjustments that might need to be made to the 1975 Luxembourg Convention in order to   **2.111** offer users a system that is accessible and legally secure at a reasonable cost. But other technical questions are raised including the further harmonisation of certain aspects of patent law that could be necessary at Community level, the impact of the information society and electronic commerce on software-related inventions, formalities, and the use of patent agents.

(b) Biotechnological patent directive

2.114 After the directive was rejected by the European Parliament, it was thought that such an act would be the end of attempts to harmonise the law on the grant of biotechnology patents in Europe. However, the Commission remained concerned that without a harmonising directive, there would be no internal market in patent biotechnological products in Europe and that therefore there would be no free movement of such goods and European research would be discouraged.

Steady progress has now been made with a new draft biotechnological directive. The Council has adopted a common position on the draft directive (*Common Position (EC) 19/98 with a view to adopting Directive 98/ . . . /EC of the European Parliament and of the Council in the legal protection of biotechnological invention* O.J. [1998] C110/17). This common position was approved by the European Parliament on May 12, 1998. It thus would seem that this draft will become law in the not too distant future.

The basic premise of the directive namely that biotechnological inventions shall be protected by national laws remains (Article 1). That basic obligation has now been made subject to the obligations of Member States pursuant to international agreement and in particular the TRIPS Agreement and the Convention on Biological Diversity pursuant to an amendment proposed by the European Parliament (Article 1(2)). The draft directive makes it clear that inventions which are otherwise patentable shall not be excluded from patentability merely because they concern a product consisting of or containing biological material or a process by means of which biological material is produced, processed or used (Article 3). "Biological material" is defined as any material containing genetic information and capable of reproducing itself or being reproduced in a biological system (Article 2(1)). The directive makes it clear that even if biological material previously occurred in nature, it is still patentable where isolated from its natural environment or produced by means of a technical process.

The directive maintains the *sui generis* protection for animal and plant varieties by excluding them *per se* from being patentable but making it clear that inventions which are not confined to a particular variety are patentable (Article 4).

Article 5 introduces a proposal made by the European Parliament who were particularly concerned about patents being taken out on genetic material occurring in human bodies. It states that the human body, at the various stages of its formation and development, and the simple discovery of one of its elements, including the sequence or partial sequence of a gene, cannot constitute patentable invention. However, an element isolated from the human body or otherwise produced by means of a technical process including the sequence or partial sequence of a gene may constitute a patentable invention. This provision highlights the distinction between a discovery (excluded from patentability) and an invention (patentable). In order to reinforce this distinction, the industrial application of a sequenced or a partial sequence of a gene must be disclosed in the patent application.

Article 6 also is a Parliament-led provision. It sets out that inventions shall not be patentable where their commercial exploitation is contrary to *ordre public* or morality. Article 6 gives examples of what this might be including processes for cloning human beings; processes for modifying the germ line genetic identity of human beings; uses of human embryos for industrial or commercial purposes and processes for modifying the genetic identity of animals which are likely to cause them suffering without any substantial medical benefit to man or animal and also animals resulting from such processes.

The protection conferred by biotechnological patents is expressed to extend to any biological material derived from that biological material through propagation or multiplication in an identical or divergent form and possessing the same characteristics. Such protection is also conferred on products which incorporate the patented genetic material and in which the genetic information is contained and performs its function.

Article 11 maintains derogations for farmers by stipulating that purchase of the patented material implies authorisation for the farmer to use the product of his harvest for multiplication and/or propagation on his own farm in a similar manner to that set out in the Community Plant Variety Rights Regulation (see para 6.019 and in particular, see 6.029).

Article 12 provides for compulsory cross-licensing upon payment of an appropriate royalty where a breeder cannot acquire or exploit a plant variety right without infringing a prior patent and vice versa where a patentee cannot exploit the patent without infringing a plant breeders' right. Where a compulsory licence is sought from the breeder or patentee, the latter is also entitled to a similar cross licence from the applicant. The applicant must demonstrate that he has unsuccessfully applied to the holder of the right and that the plant variety or invention constitutes "significant technical progress of considerable economic interest compared with the invention claimed in the [respectively] patent or the protected plant variety".

Finally, the draft directive makes various provisions about the deposit, access and re-deposit of biological material which is to form the subject of the patent application (Article 13).

(c) Supplementary protection for patented pharmaceutical products

2.115   *Introduction*—After "Importantly, there is a pending application by Spain to declare the regulation void as misuse of the European Treaty", add:

In C–350/92, *Kingdom of Spain v. Council of the European Union* [1996] C.M.L.R. 415; [1996] F.S.R. 73, Spain challenged the *vires* of the SPC regulation. The Regulation was passed by a qualified majority in the Council taking as its legal basis Article 100a of the EEC Treaty. Spain argued that: (i) the Community did not have competence to legislate to create a new patent right relying in particular upon Articles 222 and 36 and (ii) in any event, Article 100a was not the correct legal basis for the Regulation since the Regulation was not a harmonising measure and did not promote the objectives of the internal market. The Court, in dismissing the application, held: (i) that Article 222 did not reserve a power to enact substantive patent law to the national legislature to the exclusion of any Community action in the matter; (ii) Article 36 of the Treaty is not designed to reserve certain matters to the exclusive jurisdiction of Member States; (iii) neither Article restricted the competence of the Community in the field of intellectual property to harmonise national laws and to create new rights superimposed upon national rights; (iv) the Regulation did not create a new right; (v) the Regulation aimed to prevent the heterogeneous development of national laws leading to disparities which would create obstacles to the free movement of products in the Community and thus was enacted in order to achieve the completion of the internal market following the objectives set out in Article 8a (7a of the post-Maastricht version of the Treaty) of the E.C. Treaty and thus validly adopted on the basis of Article 100a of the Treaty. See also para 1.034A of this Supplement.

2.116   In *Biogen Inc v. SmithKline Beecham Biological SA* [1997] R.P.C. 833 (ECJ), it was held that where a product is protected by a number of basic patents in force which belong to a number of patent holders, each of those patents could be designated for the purpose of the procedure for the grant of an SPC. However, only one SPC could be granted for each basic patent.

Furthermore, it was held that where the owner of the marketing authorisation was different to the owner of the basic patent, the former is not required to provide the patent holder with a copy of that authorisation but in such circumstances, it was not proper to refuse an SPC on that ground alone. The national authority responsible for granting SPCs could obtain a copy of the marketing authorisation from the national authority which issued it.

2.119   In *Farmitalia Carlo Erba Srl's SPC Application* [1996] R.P.C. 111, the proprietor of the basic patent protecting the drug cabergoline applied for an SPC. Authorisation to market the product in respect of human use only had been granted pursuant to Directive 65/65/EEC and the first authorisation to place the product on the market in the Community in respect of human use was stated to be a Netherlands authorisation dated October 21, 1992. However, the applicant drew attention to an Italian authorisation dated January 7, 1987 under Directive 81/851/EEC for the sale of a veterinary medicine containing cabergoline for marketed veterinary use only. The applicant argued that the relevant date "of first authorisation to place the product on the market in the Community" as set out by Article 13(1) should be that of the Netherlands date. The applicant argued that it was necessary to have regard to the intention of the SPC Regulation before applying literally the words of Article 13. Thus, if an application for an SPC was based upon an authorisation order *for human use* in a Member State, the relevant date under Article 13 should be the date when the product protected by the basic patent was first authorised to be put on the market in the Community *for human use*. However, the Patent Office did not accept this argument and held that the meaning of Article 13 was clear—the relevant date was the first authorisation to place the product on the market for *any* use.

In *Yamanouchi Pharmaceuticals Co. Ltd v. Comptroller-General* [1997]   2.123
R.P.C. 844 (referred to in Footnote 44), the licensee of an applicant for an SPC in the United Kingdom for a drug called eformoterol for the treatment of asthma had obtained marketing authorisation in France for the solution aerosol formulation but had been refused marketing authorisation in the United Kingdom. The application was based on the transitional provisions of Article 19. The Patent Office refused the application on the grounds that no marketing authorisation had been obtained in the United Kingdom as required by Article 3 of the Regulation set out in para. 2.116 of the book.

The matter went to the ECJ—C–110/95 *Yamanouchi Pharmaceuticals Co. Ltd v. Comptroller-General of Patents, Designs and Trade Marks* [1997] 3 C.M.L.R. 749. It held that Article 19(1) could not be construed as meaning that the existence of an authorisation in the Member State in which the SPC was sought was of no relevance. The grant of an SPC pursuant to the transitional provisions of Article 19 was conditional on a valid authorisation to place the product on the market as a medicinal product having been granted in the Member State in which the application was submitted and which was existing at the date of that application.

In *Draco AB's SPC Application* [1996] R.P.C. 417 (English High Court), the owner of a patent for the anti-asthmatic drug budesonide applied for an SPC for "additive-free budesonide in the form of agglomerated micronised particles" (*i.e.* budesonide in a powder form). Product licences had been obtained for it in Denmark in 1989 and in the United Kingdom in 1990. However, in 1981 and 1982, product licences had been obtained in the United Kingdom for budesonide suspended in an aerosol propellant.

In an argument over the relevant starting date for the SPC, the applicant argued that the product (defined as the active ingredient—see para. 2.117) was the powder form of budesonide. Accordingly, authorisations for the aerosol formulation were irrelevant. However, both the Patent Office and, on appeal, the High Court rejected this argument. They both stated that in interpreting the SPC Regulation, the active ingredient was budesonide and not a particular formulation of it.

2.124A   *EPC and regulation*—A Regulation providing for a Supplementary Protection Certificate for plant protection products was adopted on June 10, 1996. At present, the final text has not yet been published.

8. COMPARISON OF NATIONAL, PCT, EPC AND HYBRID ROUTES

(a) Obtaining patents in Europe: comparison of routes

(iii) Application under the EPC

2.133   *Merits and disadvantages*—In a recent study on fees, the EPO recorded that a European patent for all contracting states would cost 12,540DM whereas national applications in all contracting states would cost 17,280DM. However, the national route would involve considerable duplication of agents' costs. Accordingly, it is clear that the national route is much more expensive.

9. TABLE OF MEMBERSHIP OF EUROPEAN COUNTRIES TO THE PARIS CONVENTION, PCT I & II, EPC AND EC

2.139   Finland and Norway have now acceded to the EPC.
    Latvia and Albania now permit the extension of European Patents to their territories. It is anticipated that Romania which has a long patenting tradition will soon become a member of the EPC.

significant part of the circles for which it is intended as a symbol for the goods which are made under it—see *Eraldo Sante Cipriai v. CPR 88* Court of Florence, October 13, 1995, summarised in [1996] 1 EIPR D–16, where the defence failed on the facts.

Portugal—Portugal has not changed its previous law that confers on a person who uses an unregistered mark a right of priority as against later applicants provided that the former has not used the mark for more than six months (Article 171). This imposes a burden on the unregistered user to apply for registration within a period of six months after beginning use failing which the user loses all rights against a later application.

Spain—Spain only protects unregistered trade names (*i.e.* the name of the business) pursuant to Article 8 of the Paris Convention. Any opposition must be brought within five years of the date of publication of the grant of registration (Article 77 Law 32/88).

Sweden—Sweden confers substantial rights on prior users of unregistered marks. Article 14 of the Trade Marks Act (as amended) confers rights to third parties where the mark is likely to deceive the public; is likely to convey the impression of being another person's trade name; is confusingly similar to a name or a trade name which is being used in the course of another person's business activities or is confusingly similar to a trade symbol which is being used at the date of application to the knowledge of the applicant and the applicant had not used the mark prior to the use of the other symbol.

(b) Scope of exclusive right

Austria has not adopted Article 5(2). Ireland , Finland and Sweden have adopted Article 5(2). Benelux has now implemented the directive. The law provides for protection against use of the mark on dissimilar goods in certain circumstances. 3.005

France has introduced an opposition procedure whereby during a period of 2 months following publication of the application for registration, any concerned person may submit observations to the national office. 3.006

3. INTERNATIONAL TREATIES

(c) The Madrid Protocol

The Madrid Protocol has now been ratified by the following European countries: Czech Republic, Germany, Norway, Denmark, Finland, Norway, Poland, Spain, Sweden and the United Kingdom. Accordingly, the Madrid Protocol is now in force. 3.019

4. COMMUNITY TRADE MARK LEGISLATION

(a) Community Trade Mark

(i) Introduction

3.031 The CTMO started business on April 1, 1996. Filings in the first year were three times that predicted. This has meant delays caused by staff shortages although more staff have been promised. The main attraction appears to be the saving in costs. The geographic origin of the applications is interesting. The countries that have filed the greatest number of applications are the USA, Spain, the United Kingdom and Germany. Other Member States of the European Union have been considerably further behind.

OHIM (Office for Harmonisation of the Internal Market) has agreed to provide all pre-advertised CTM application data (including full goods/services specifications) to search agencies.

There are now two supplementary regulations: Commission Regulation 2868/95 which is the Implementing Regulation containing the rules governing the procedure for obtaining a CTM and Regulation 2869/95 which is the Fees Regulation. An example of the fees are as follows: basic fee for application for registration of a CTM in respect of a maximum of three classes of goods and services — 975 ECU; opposition fee — 350 ECU; basic fee for the registration of a CTM in respect of three classes of goods and services — 1,100 ECU; basic fee for the renewal of a CTM — 2,500 ECU; fee for an application for the revocation of a CTM — 700 ECU and appeal fee — 800 ECU. Both Regulations can be found at [1995] O.J. L303. OHIM has also produced Examination Guidelines which can be obtained on request.

A copy of the CTM regulation can be found at [1995] OJOHIM 50.

(iii) Substantive law

3.034 *Types of CTM* — FOOTNOTE 4: Add: This may include registration for a single colour or a combination of colours or a sound — see *Joint Statement by Council and Commission entered in the Minutes of the Council Meeting at which the CTM Regulation was adopted on December 20, 1993* [1996] OJOHIM 613.

At end of paragraph, add: The Council and the Commission do not consider the activity of retail trading in goods is a service for which a CTM may be registered under the regulation — see *Joint Statement by Council and Commission entered in the Minutes of the Council Meeting at which the CTM Regulation was adopted on December 20, 1993* [1996] OJOHIM 613.

3.036 *Absolute grounds for refusal* — Where footnote 6 refers to the relevance of the italicised section, the italicisation of the relevant text has been omitted in the printing stage. The italics should start from "trade marks devoid of distinctive character" to "bona fide and established practices of the trade".

Vincent O'Reilly, Head of the Examination Division of OHIM, has intimated that surnames would not be refused registration unless they were *prima facie* objectionable for other reasons—FARMER for agricultural goods. He stated that descriptiveness in only one language of the possible 11 Community languages would create an obstacle to registration. Where the applicant is relying upon acquired distinctiveness, the applicant must supply evidence from the territory where the mark is distinctive.

The reference to "shape of goods" is also intended to cover the three dimensional form of goods (*Joint Statement by Council and Commission entered in the Minutes of the Council Meeting at which the CTM Regulation was adopted on December 20, 1993* [1996] OJOHIM 613).

The Opposition Division has now published some decisions in opposition proceedings.   3.037

In *Decision No. 16/1998 ARISTON/HORIZON* [1998] OJOHIM 719, the Opposition Division held that the marks Horizon and Ariston were not confusingly similar in relation to cigarettes.

In *Decision No. 20/1998 HUMICA/HUMIC* [1998] OJOHIM 733, the application was for the mark HUMIC for *inter alia* chemicals used in horticulture and forestry and fertilizers. The Opponent owned the Portuguese device mark "HUMICA" for organic fertilizers. The Opposition Division held that as chemicals used in horticulture and forestry would have a similar function and are likely to be distributed and sold in the same kind of stores and shops as organic fertilizers and intended for the same public, they were similar goods. The marks were held to be confusingly similar. In particular, the Opposition Division held that from an intellectual/conceptual point of view, the two marks are to be considered similar. It held that although the opponent's mark was a device mark, the similarities were marked and comparison of two marks should be based on their points of similarity and not their differences. In *Decision No. 7/1998 BEAUTY FREE* [1998] OJOHIM 659, dentrifices were held not to be similar goods to preparations for body care. The two marks "BEAUTY FREE" and device mark with fancy font "BEAUTY FREE SHOP" were held to be confusingly similar for cosmetics and similar products.

Rights of CTM proprietors—The Council and Commission have   3.038
noted that the reference to "likelihood of association" is a concept which has in particular been developed by Benelux law—*Joint Statement by Council and Commission entered in the Minutes of the Council Meeting at which the CTM Regulation was adopted on December 20, 1993* [1996] OJOHIM 613 at 615. However, note that in relation to the directive, a similar statement by the Council and Commission was not

accepted as being applicable in the United Kingdom (see para. 3.073). The ECJ has now ruled on the meaning of likelihood of association in the context of the Trade Mark Directive in *Sabel v. Puma* (discussed below at para. 3.073).

FOOTNOTE 17: Add: The Council and the Commission consider that the reference to advertising in paragraph 2(d) does not cover the use of a CTM in comparative advertising—*Joint Statement by Council and Commission entered in the Minutes of the Council Meeting at which the CTM Regulation was adopted on December 20, 1993* [1996] OJOHIM 613 at 615.

3.039 *Defences of third parties*—The defence of using one's own name is considered by the Council and Commission to only apply in respect of natural persons—*Joint Statement by Council and Commission entered in the Minutes of the Council Meeting at which the CTM Regulation was adopted on December 20, 1993* [1996] OJOHIM 613 at 615.

3.042 *Licensing*—A licensee may only bring proceedings against a third party if the licence is registered (see Article 23(1)).

3.043 *Collective marks*—See Rules 42 and 43 of Regulation 2868/95 which set out the procedure for applying for a Community collective mark.

FOOTNOTE 33: Add: The Council and Commission consider that a collective mark which is available for use only by members of an association which owns the mark is liable to mislead if it gives the impression that it is available for use by anyone who is able to meet certain objective standards—*Joint Statement by Council and Commission entered in the Minutes of the Council Meeting at which the CTM Regulation was adopted on December 20, 1993* [1996] OJOHIM 607 at 619.

(iv) Procedural law

3.045 *Application for CTM*—FOOTNOTE 38: Add: See also Rules 1 to 3 of E.C. Regulation 2868/95 [1995] OJOHIM 259 (the Implementing Regulation of the CTM) which gives further details as to what is required on the application form. A *pro forma* application form is available from the CTMO and is published at [1996] OJOHIM 7. It is not mandatory but its use is strongly recommended.

At end of paragraph, add: The fees payable for the application will consist of the basic fee and a class fee for each class exceeding three to which the goods or services belong—Rule 4 E.C. Regulation 2868/95.

3.045A Insert as new paragraph:

Representation before CTMO—Natural or legal persons who have their domicile or their principal place of business or a real and effective industrial or commercial establishment in the Community may represent themselves (Article 88(1) and [1995] OJOHIM 17). If this condition is not satisfied, an agent must be appointed to act on their behalf (Article 88(2)). A limited exception to this rule is provided where employees of legal persons within the Community may also represent other legal persons from outside the Community when there are economic connections between the two legal persons such as common ownership or control (Article 88(3)).

Only legal practitioners or professional representatives entered on the CTMO register may act as agents before the CTMO ([1995] OJOHIM 17). The legal practitioner must be qualified in a Member State, have his place of business in the Community and be entitled to act as a representative in trade mark matters. In order to be placed on the CTMO register as a qualified person, the representative must be a national of a Member State, have his place of business in the Community and be entitled to represent natural or legal persons in trade mark matters in the central industrial property office of the Member State where he has employment (Article 89(2)). For further details, see *Communication No. 1/95 of the President of the Office of September 18, 1995 on professional representation* [1995] OJOHIM 17.

Priority—Vincent O'Reilly, Head of the Examination Division of OHIM, has said that a claim to seniority can only be made where the senior mark is registered at the date of application for a CTM. It is impermissible for the prior national right to be pending on that date. See also Rules 6 to 9 of Regulation 2868/95 (the Implementing Regulation) as to further details on how to claim priority.   3.046

FOOTNOTE 44: Add: See also Rule 28, Regulation 2868/95.

Examination—After first sentence, add: If the application fails to meet the requirements for according a filing date because it does not contain: a request for registration of the mark; information identifying the applicant; a list of goods or services for which the mark is to be registered; a representation of the mark or if the basic fee is not paid within one month of the filing of the application, the application is deficient and the CTMO will notify the applicant or his agent that a filing date cannot be conferred—Rule 9, Regulation 2868/95. If the deficiencies are remedied within two months of receipt of the notification, the application will be deemed to have been filed when such deficiencies have been remedied otherwise the application will fail. In respect of other deficiencies, the CTMO will give the applicant a period in which to remedy them (Rule 9(3), Regulation 2868/95).   3.047

At end of paragraph, add: Mr O'Reilly, Head of the Examination Division of OHIM, has said that it will not entertain *ex parte* hearings on questions of registrability.

FOOTNOTE 48: Add: A fee of 25 ECU will be charged for each national search report carried out—[1995] OJOHIM (*Official Journal of the Office for Harmonisation of the Internal Market*) 15.

FOOTNOTE 49: Add: See also Rule 12, Regulation 2868/95 [1995] OJOHIM 280.

3.047A   Insert as new paragraph:

Amendment of CTM application—A CTM application may be amended upon request of the applicant only by correcting the name and address of the applicant, errors of wording or of copying or obvious mistakes provided that such correction does not substantially change the trade mark or extend the list of goods or services—Article 44 CTM Regulation and Rules 13, 14, Regulation 2868/95.

3.048   For a detailed guide to the Opposition procedure in the CTM system, see *Gevers and Tatham* [1998] EIPR 22. See also *CTMO's Guidelines on Opposition Proceedings* [1997] OJOHIM 1019.

Opposition—FOOTNOTE 50: Add: See also Rules 14 and 15, Regulation 2868/95 for details concerning the procedure in bringing an opposition.

After "brought by third parties", add: Where the notice of opposition is based on an earlier mark which is not a CTM, the notice of opposition should include evidence of registration. If the opposition is based on a well-known mark, the notice of opposition should be accompanied by evidence attesting that it is well known or that it has a reputation. If the opposition is entered on the basis of any other earlier right, the notice should be accompanied by appropriate evidence on the acquisition and scope of protection of that right—see Rule 16, Regulation 2868/95.

At end of paragraph, add: See Rules 19 to 22, Regulation 2868/95 regarding the procedure involved in opposition hearings.

A failure to set out the grounds of opposition is fatal—*Decision No. 1/1997 INSTRALUBE/IRGALUBE* [1998] OJOHIM 711.

3.049   *Languages*—FOOTNOTE 57: Add: Also any application or declaration relating to a CTM application may be filed in the language used for filing the CTM application or in the second language—Rule 95(1), Regulation 2868/95. A failure to provide a translation of a Notice of Opposition into either the language of filing or the second language within one month from the expiry of the opposition period is fatal—*Decision No. 6/1997 PROFIL* [1998] OJOHIM 653.

At end of first paragraph, add: Generally, in written proceedings before the CTMO, any party may use any official language of the CTMO. However, if that language is not the language of the proceedings, a translation into that language must be provided within one month of the date of submission of the original document. If the applicant is the sole party to proceedings and the language used for filing the application was not a CTMO language, the translation may be provided in the second language indicated in the application—see Rule 96(1), Regulation

2868/95. Thus, in *Decision No. 16/1998 ARISTON* [1998] OJOHIM 719, the opponent failed to translate evidence into the language of the proceedings, the CTMO refused to take account of it.

FOOTNOTE 58: Add: See also Rule 17, Regulation 2868/95.

FOOTNOTE 59: Add: See also Rule 95(b), Regulation 2868/95 which provides that an application or declaration relating to a registered CTM may be filed in one of the languages of the Office.

Insert as new paragraph: 3.049A

Registration—Assuming that there have been no adverse findings against the application, a certificate of registration is issued and the registration published in the CTM Bulletin. A registration fee consisting of a basic fee and a class fee for each class exceeding three in respect of which the mark is to be registered must be paid (see Rules 23, 24, Regulation 2868/95).

Insert as new paragraph: 3.049B

Fees—The CTMO has now published the fees payable in an application for registration. The main categories are set out below (see Article 2, Rules on Fees [1995] OJOHIM 415 at 419).

Basic fee for application	975 ECU
Fee for each class over 3	200 ECU
Basic fee for application for collective mark	1675 ECU
Fee for each class over 3 in collective marks	400 ECU
Opposition fee	350 ECU
Fee for alteration of representation of mark	200 ECU
Basic fee for registration of mark	1100 ECU
Fee for each class over 3 (at registration stage)	200 ECU
Basic fee for registration of collective mark	2200 ECU
Fee for each class over 3 (for collective mark at registration)	400 ECU
Basic fee for renewal of mark	2500 ECU
Fee for each class over 3 (at renewal)	500 ECU
Basic fee for renewal of collective mark	5000 ECU
Fee for each class over 3 (of collective mark at renewal)	1000 ECU
Fee for application for revocation or declaration of invalidity	700 ECU
Appeal fee	800 ECU
Fee for *restitutio in integrum*	200 ECU
Fee for conversion of CTM into national mark	200 ECU

Duration and renewal of CTM—The CTMO will inform the   3.050
proprietor of a CTM six months prior to its expiry that the registration

is approaching expiry—Rule 29, Regulation 2868/95. Applications for renewal are governed by Rule 30.

3.051 *Revocation of CTM*—FOOTNOTE 62: Add: The Council and the Commission consider that use which is genuine use in one Member State is genuine use in the Community—*Joint Statement by Council and Commission entered in the Minutes of the Council Meeting at which the CTM Regulation was adopted on December 20, 1993* [1996] OJOHIM 613 at 615. Article 15 uses the same wording as Article 50(1)(a) but does not specifically relate to grounds for revocation. Note that use with the consent of the proprietor is deemed use by the proprietor (Article 15(3)).

FOOTNOTE 64: Add: See also Rules 39 to 41, Regulation 2868/95 for the procedure governing applications for revocation or declaration of invalidity.

3.052 *General provisions as to conduct of proceedings before the CTMO*—See also Rules 52 to 60, Regulation 2868/95 which set out further details regarding general provisions as to the conduct of proceedings before the CTMO. In oral proceedings, any party to proceedings may in place of the language of the proceedings, use any language of the CTMO on condition that there is provision for interpretation into the language of the proceedings. The applicant may in oral proceedings concerning an application for registration use the language of the application or his second language—Rule 97(1), Regulation 2868/95.

3.053 *Division of jurisdiction between CTMO and courts of Member States*—FOOTNOTE 80: Add: The Council and the Commission consider that the aim of Article 90(1) is to render the Brussels Convention applicable to the Regulation insofar as the provisions of the Regulation do not derogate therefrom—*Joint Statement by Council and Commission entered in the Minutes of the Council Meeting at which the CTM Regulation was adopted on December 20, 1993* [1996] OJOHIM 607 at 621.

3.057 *Appeals*—The procedure governing appeals is set out in Rules 48 to 51, Regulation 2868/95. An appeal fee is required although this will be reimbursed if such reimbursement is equitable by reason of a substantial procedural violation (Rule 51). See also E.C. Regulation 216/96 laying down the rules of procedure of the Boards of Appeal—[1996] OJOHIM 399.

3.058 *Conversion of CTM registration or application into national trade mark application*—The procedure for converting a CTM application or registration into a national application or registration is governed by Rules 44 to 47, Regulation 2868/95.

(vi) Merits of CTM over national trade marks and International trade mark (the Madrid Agreement and its Protocol)

As mentioned in this paragraph, the main advantage of the CTM is that **3.060** it saves costs. In fact, this appears to be a decisive factor and has convinced many applicants to file for a CTM with the resultant fact that three times the number of applications have been received as were expected in its first year of operation. Approximately, the saving is £3,000 via the CTM route as opposed to £15,000 via the national route.

Another advantage of the CTM route is that use of the mark in one Member State will be sufficient to prevent an application for revocation of the mark for non-use from succeeding.

(b) First Trade Mark Harmonisation Directive 89/104

(ii) Structure and contents of directive

The Council and Commission adopted statements for entry in the Min- **3.062** utes of the Council Meeting at which the directive was adopted. In *Wagamama v. City Centre Restaurants plc* [1995] F.S.R. 713, Mr Justice Laddie held that these minutes could not be used in order to construe a directive. However, see also Gielen, "European Trade Mark Legislation: The Statements" [1996] EIPR 83 where the author argues to the contrary.

(iii) Signs of which a trade mark may consist

The Council and Commission consider that registration for a single **3.063** colour or a combination of colours or a sound is possible—see *Joint Statement by Council and Commission entered in the Minutes of the Council Meeting at which the CTM Regulation was adopted on December 20, 1993* [1996] OJOHIM 607.

(iv) Grounds for refusal or invalidity

(1) Absolute grounds for refusal

Mandatory grounds

The Council and Commission do not consider that the expression **3.064** "devoid of any distinctive character" adds anything more to the definition of a trade mark, namely that it must be capable of distinguishing the goods or services of one undertaking from another—see *Joint Statement by Council and Commission entered in the Minutes of the Council Meeting at which the CTM Regulation was adopted on December 20, 1993* [1996] OJOHIM 607.

Decisions in Member States countries on the absolute registrability of marks based on domestic legislation enacted to bring into force the Directive are beginning to emerge.

The Netherlands—In *Bio-Claire Int. v. Benelux Trade Marks Office* [1998] ETMR 251, the Court of Appeal at the Hague, Netherlands, held that the phrase "BIO-CLAIRE" for cleaning materials and detergents, granules, powders, liquids and other material for removing algae from ponds was devoid of distinctive character for the goods for which it was registered. The Court said "the acceptance of BIO-CLAIRE as a trade mark would prevent third parties describing similar goods and services with this combination of words. In brief, BIO-CLAIRE did not have such an individual character as to make it suitable to distinguish the goods and services under this mark from similar goods and services and to demonstrate sufficiently the origin of any given concern". Furthermore, it held that use of the mark did not render it factually distinctive.

Austria—The Supreme Court held that the mark "XTC Ecstasy" for non-alcoholic beverages was not devoid of distinctive character (*XTC Trade Mark* [1998] ETMR 268)

Germany—In *"Tax Free Trade Mark Application"* [1998] ETMR 193, the Bundespatentgericht held that a device mark which contained the words "Tax Free for Tourists" in bright colours and depicted within a double lined square for advertising and business services in connection with the refund of value added tax paid by tourists was registrable as the registration could not prevent the usage by others of the words alone. See also the decision of Bundespatentgericht in *Ergopanel Trade Mark Application* [1997] ETMR 495 where it was held that "Ergopanel" was not registrable in respect of goods which would have or use control consoles. In *Bonus TM Application* [1997] ETMR 413, it was held that the word BONUS was not registrable for a range of goods because it consisted exclusively of a sign which was customary in many areas of trade.

United Kingdom—In *British Sugar plc v. James Robertson* [1996] R.P.C. 281, Mr Justice Jacob held that under the Trade Marks Act 1994 which enacts the Directive, "Treat" in relation to syrups was devoid of distinctive character; consisted exclusively of a sign which may serve in trade to designate the kind, quality and intended purpose of the produce and was a sign which had become customary in the current language.

The UK Trade Marks Registry refused an application for "Weblink" for computer software for use in connection with the internet on the grounds that it was devoid of distinctive character in the absence of distinctive character acquired through use—*Lombard Document Systems Limited's Application* [1997] ETMR 500. See also *BOCM Pauls Ltd and Scottish Agricultural College's Application* [1997] ETMR 420;

[1997] R.P.C. 279 where it was held on appeal from the Trade Mark Registry that "Eurolamb" was not registrable for lamb carcasses and meat because it was devoid of distinctive character and descriptive of the goods themselves contrary to domestic provisions which equated to Article 3(1)(b) and 3(1)(c) of the Directive. See also *Warnaco's Inc Application* [1997] ETMR 505 where "THE PERFECTIONISTS" was held devoid of distinctive character for articles of underclothing as it was merely laudatory (the mark had been accepted in Denmark) . In *Allied Domecq PLC's Application* [1997] ETMR 253, it was held on appeal from the Trade Marks Registry that the mark "AD2000" was devoid of distinctive character as it was a mark which " . . . it cannot rightly be said to be incapable of fair and honest application to the goods of anyone other than the applicant" and did not have the capacity to "communicate the fact" that if used on certain goods it would denote that such goods were from one and the same undertaking.

In *Philips v. Remington* [1998] ETMR 124; Mr Justice Jacob held that a mark which consisted of a graphical image of the three headed shaver of the well known Philishave was devoid of distinctive character. He considered that the mark primarily denoted function. Greater use of the sign would not make any difference. The sign could never denote shavers made by Phillips rather than someone else because it primarily says "here is a three headed shaver". Thus, he held that it was not "capable" of denoting only Phillips goods. There was evidence about the fact the public recognised the three headed shaver as being a Phillips shaver. However, Jacob J quoted from Hoffmann J in *Unilever (Striped Toothpaste No. 2) TM* [1987] R.P.C. 19 where the judge said that

> "There is in my view a similar obstacle in the path of a trader who has enjoyed a *de facto* monopoly of a product with a relatively simple feature chosen not as a badge of origin but on the grounds that it was likely to appeal to the public. The fact that members of the public now associate that feature with its product tells one nothing about what they would think if a product with a similar feature came upon the market".

Sweden—In *Ide Line Aktiebolag v. Philips Electronics N.V.* Case No. T7–1316–94; T7–249–97 [1997] ETMR 377, the Swedish courts had to determine exactly the same issue as in the English *Phillips v. Remington* case described above. The Swedish court held that the trade mark depicting the three headed shaver was distinctive of Phillips contrary to the UK court's finding.

Secondary meaning—**United Kingdom**—In *British Sugar v. Robertson* [1996] R.P.C. 281 at 306, Mr Justice Jacob held that in the case of common or apt descriptive or laudatory words, compelling evidence is needed to establish secondary meaning and that, in particular, mere

3.065

evidence of extensive use would be unlikely to be enough on its own. Thus, where the mark was "Treat", it must be shown that the mark had really become accepted by a substantial majority of persons as a trade mark, *i.e.* is or is almost a household word.

The meaning of Article 3(1)(e) ("signs which consist exclusively of (i) the shape which results from the nature of the goods themselves or (ii) the shape of goods which is necessary to obtain a technical result or (iii) the shape which gives substantial value to the goods") has been the subject of decisions of two Member States: Sweden and England. Both concerned the registrability of a mark which represented graphically the well-known shape of the three headed rotary Phillips shaver. In Sweden, in *Ide Line Aktiebolag v. Philips Electronics N.V.* Case No. T7–1316-94; T7–249-97 [1997] ETMR 377, the Stockholm District Court held that the trade mark was validly registered and could not be said to be necessary to obtain the technical result since the result—the shaving of hair by means of a rotary cutter—could be achieved without any considerable change in cost or efficiency by the use of a number of different shaving heads of different dimensions and equipped with a different number of cutters. However, Judge Goran Nilsson dissented in this case saying that there are two ways of interpreting Article 3(1)(e). The first is that the provision relates "only to such technical result which is expected to be reached with the shape to the extent that there is no obstacle for registration when an equal result can be obtained with another shape". He said that another way to interpret the provision is to make a "total analysis of the elements of the shape of the product and consider whether these are caused by purely technical reasons in relation to the result which is desired." Nilsson preferred the latter approach considering the former approach unduly restrictive of free movement of goods and not likely to have been intended. He said that the provision should be interpreted to be a bar to registration of trade marks where the shape is solely motivated by the technical result even if there were alternative means to reach that result.

In England, in the parallel case on the same facts, *Phillips v. Remington* [1998] ETMR 124; [1998] R.P.C. 283 (High Court of England), Jacob J found that the mark was devoid of distinctive character (discussed in para. 3.064). In considering the Article 3(1)(e) defences, he held that:

(a) the sign did not consist exclusively of the shape which resulted from the nature of the goods themselves. Jacob J said the defence raised the question of the level of specificity that a court should define the goods. Thus, one could define the goods as three headed rotary shavers or just electric shavers. He decided that the question must be answered from a practical business view and held that the goods were regarded as electric shavers. Accordingly, he held that the defence was not made out.

(b) In considering whether the shape of goods were necessary to give a technical result, he quoted from the judgments in the Swedish case and preferred the dissenting judgment of Judge Nilsson. He considered that the majority viewpoint gave the provision no or almost no scope at all because one can hardly think of any object which must be of a particular shape to perform a function.

(c) In considering whether the shape gave substantial value to the goods, he upheld this defence. He considered that Phillips had consistently relied upon the advantages of their rotary shaver as being efficient and effective. Thus, he held that the three-headed shape is recognised as having an engineering function and thus added substantial value to the product.

United Kingdom—In *Kundry SA's Application* [1998] ETMR 178, the 3.066 Trade Marks Registry quoted from parliamentary material used while the Trade Marks Bill was before Parliament that examples where bad faith might be found are:

"where the applicant was aware that someone else intended to use and/or register the mark, particularly where the applicant has a relationship for example as employee or agent, with that other person, or where the applicant has copied a mark being used abroad with the intention of pre-empting the proprietor who intends to trade in the United Kingdom."

Germany—The Bundespatentgericht in *Absperrpoller Trade Mark Application* [1997] ETMR 176 has permitted the grant of a trade mark for a two dimensional representation of a traffic bollard where the bollard was a distinctive bollard designed with a nostalgic effect and not a simple bollard. The Court held that under the new Trade Mark law, shape marks could be given protection and it could not be said that the shape of the bollard was derived from the nature of the goods themselves.

England—In the *Ever Ready TM* Decision of the Trade Marks Registry 3.068 6.4.1998 (unreported), the Hearing Officer considered an application for the mark "Eveready" for condoms and the opposition to that mark by Ever Ready Ltd who made and sold "Ever Ready" batteries. He considered that Article 4(4)(a) is aimed at protecting against illegitimate exploitation of the reputation of a mark. He said that the reputation that a trade mark enjoys is very much dependent on its ability to function as an indication of origin. However, he said that it did not necessarily follow that another trade mark can only take unfair advantage, or cause detriment to, the repute of another trade mark as a result of confusion as to origin. He noted that if the framers of the directive had intended to introduce the requirement of confusion, it was strange that they chose not to. He thus concluded that confusion was not a requirement of Article 4(4)(a).

In considering the concepts of unfair advantage and detriment to the distinctive character or repute of the mark, the Hearing Officer held that no unfair advantage had been taken because there was no conceptual confusion between their reputation for batteries and condoms. In considering whether or not it was detrimental to the distinctive character of the opponent's mark, the Hearing Officer said that any use of the same or similar mark is liable to some extent to dilute the distinctiveness of the earlier mark. The provision could not have been intended to have the sweeping effect of preventing the registration of any mark which is the same as or similar to, a trade mark with a reputation. He considered that it was appropriate to consider the following matters: the inherent distinctiveness of the earlier trade mark; the extent of the reputation that the earlier mark enjoys; the range of goods for which the earlier mark enjoys a reputation; the uniqueness or otherwise of the mark in the market place; whether the respective goods/services although dissimilar, are in some way related or likely to be sold through the same outlets; whether the earlier trade mark will be any less distinctive for the goods/services for which it has a reputation than it was before.

He furthermore held that in the 1990s, in the era of safe sex, little embarrassment arose from the use of the mark for condoms and it was fanciful that the opponent's mark would become the butt of misplaced humour or even ridicule.

(v) Rights conferred by a trade mark

Mandatory provisions

3.069   *Rights*—England—In *British Sugar plc v. James Robertson & Sons Ltd* [1996] R.P.C. 281, it was held that there was no requirement that the defendant's use of the sign in the course of trade be use in a trade mark sense (*cf.* position under Trade Marks Act 1938).

In *Trebor Bassett Ltd v. The Football Association* [1997] F.S.R. 211, the English High Court was concerned with the issue of infringement of the English "three lions" logo which was a registered trademark. It was alleged that this had been infringed by a manufacturer of candy sticks whose packaging included insert cards containing the photographs of famous footballers including members of the English national team who displayed on the national strip the "three lions" logo. Thus, the registered trade mark appeared on the cards as part of the team shirt worn by the player. The judge held the reproduction of the player's photograph inevitably reproduced the defendant's trade mark but that such reproduction was not even arguably "using" the registered mark in respect of the cards. Furthermore, by publishing and marketing such cards, the defendant was not in any real sense affixing the sign to the cards nor publishing them.

This case demonstrates that although the directive does not specifically mention that for infringement to be established there must be shown that use must be use as a trade mark, the requirement that there "be use of the sign in the course of trade in relation to the goods or services" for which protection is sought does involve consideration of whether the sign is being used to identify the trade origin of a product (in this case, collector's cards) or is merely incidental to such a product (*i.e.* because the product incidentally contains a photograph of the sign). Recently, in *Phillips v. Remington* [1998] ETMR 124, Jacob J. invited submissions that his observations that one need not show use as a trade mark in *British Sugar v. Robertson* were not necessarily correct. He declined to decide the issue but it is open for others to argue this in the future. In such a case, the case of *Trebor Bassett Limited v. The Football Association* may be of assistance *i.e.* use as a trade is implicit in use "in relation to the goods or services."

Defences—The defence of using one's own name is considered by the   3.070
Council and Commission to apply only to natural persons—see *Joint Statement by Council and Commission entered in the Minutes of the Council Meeting at which the CTM Regulation was adopted on December 20, 1993* [1996] OJOHIM 607 at 609.

In *Phillips v. Remington* [1998] ETMR 124; [1998] R.P.C. 283 (High Court of England) (discussed above in para 3.064 and 3.065), the English High Court considered a defence under Article 6.1 that the trade mark depicting a graphical image of a three headed razor merely indicated the kind and quality of the product. The court upheld that defence (although it was not necessary because it had found the mark invalid).

In *BMW v. Deenik* [1998] ETMR 348, Deenik sold second hand BMW cars and also provided a repair and maintenance service for BMWs. BMW was registered for motor vehicles and parts and accessories but not for services relating to repair and maintenance of cars. The issue referred to the ECJ was whether a statement "Specialist in BMWs" or "specialised in BMWs" or "Repairs and maintenance of BMWs" constituted trade mark infringement of the BMW trade mark. Advocate-General Jacobs has advised as follows:

(a) advertisement that second-sale BMW vehicles are on sale constitutes use of the mark in relation to cars within the meaning of Article 5(1)(a) of the Directive.

(b) Article 7 of the Directive prevents a trade mark owner from exercising his rights unless such advertising seriously damages the reputation of BMW or if there is a genuine and properly substantiated likelihood that the public will be led to believe that Mr Deenik is authorised by BMW to sell cars.

(c) Article 6(1) precludes the owner of a trade mark from preventing the use of his mark by an independent trader to advertise repair and servicing of the goods covered by the mark provided that the independent trader does so in accordance with honest practices in industrial or commercial matters. It is not contrary to honest practices merely to derive advantage from the use of a mark but such would be contrary to honest practices if it leads the public to believe that the reseller is authorised by the trade mark owner or would seriously damage the reputation of the trade mark.

Optional provisions

3.071 *Rights*—England—In *Baywatch Production Co Inc v. The Home Video Channel* [1997] F.S.R. 22, the English High Court held that the domestic provision of Article 5(2) (s.10(3) Trade Marks Act 1994) only applied where there existed a likelihood of confusion between the two marks. The judge said that in his judgment, s.10(3) only applied where:

(a) A sign which is similar to the trade mark so that there is a likelihood of confusion on the part of the public, is used in relation to goods and services which are not similar to the mark.

(b) The mark has a reputation in the United Kingdom.

(c) The use of the sign, being without due cause, takes advantage of, or is detrimental to the distinctive character or the repute of the trade mark.

In doing so, the judge considered the unreported decision of Knox J in *BASF Plc v. CEP (U.K.) Plc* October 29, 1995 where the judge said that neither the distinctive character nor the repute of the plaintiff's mark is adversely affected when there is no risk of relevant confusion.

However, in *Sabel v. Puma* C–251/95 [1998] ETMR 1; [1998] R.P.C. 199; [1998] 1 C.M.L.R. 445 (discussed below), the European Court of Justice has remarked *obiter dicta* that Article 5(2) does not require proof of likelihood of confusion. Thus, in *Marks & Spencer plc v. One in a Million Ltd* [1998] F.S.R. 265, the court considered that the proper interpretation of the English provision implementing Article 5(2) was in some doubt.

See however the decision of the Trade Marks Registry in *Ever Ready TM*, Decision of April 6, 1998 (unreported) discussed above at 3.068 where the same wording is discussed in relation to Article 4(4)(a) and where it was held that likelihood of confusion need not be proved. In the author's submission, this decision is to be preferred as the importation of "likelihood of confusion" into Article 5(2) is clearly a gloss on its wording.

As to whether repackaging will constitute an act of infringement, see para. 3.075 below.

FOOTNOTE 50: Add: The Council and Commission consider that the prohibition on advertising does not affect the national provisions concerning the possibility of using or not using a trade mark in comparative advertising—*Joint Statement by Council and Commission entered in the Minutes of the Council Meeting at which the CTM Regulation was adopted on December 20, 1993* [1996] OJOHIM 607 at 609. N.B. In the United Kingdom, the Trade Marks Act 1994 which implements the Directive now permits comparative advertising provided it is not contrary to honest commercial practice whereas before, under the 1938 Act, comparative advertising was not permissible.

Defences—The Council and Commission consider that national   3.072
authorities are entitled to decide whether a proprietor has lost his entitlement to sue for other circumstances even though the acquiescence period is less than five years—*Joint Statement by Council and Commission entered in the Minutes of the Council Meeting at which the CTM Regulation was adopted on December 20, 1993* [1996] OJOHIM 607 at 609.

Comment—After first paragraph, add: In *British Sugar plc v. James*   3.073
Robertson [1996] R.P.C. 281, Mr Justice Jacob held that Trade Marks Act 1994, s. 11(2) which enacts Article 6 and is virtually identical in wording does not cover the case where a word is prima facie descriptive if, when used, it is used as a trade mark for the defendant's goods (at p. 299).

Similarity of goods

After "if the decision would affect trade between Member States" at top of p. 168, add:

England—In *British Sugar plc v. James Robertson* [1996] R.P.C. 281, Mr Justice Jacob held that the class of similar goods in s. 10(2) of the Trade Marks Act 1994 which enacted Article 5(1)(a) was a narrow one and approximated to the test of "goods of the same description" under s. 12(1) of the Trade Marks Act 1938. Relevant factors for consideration were a comparison of the use, users and physical nature of the plaintiff's and defendant's goods, the way in which they were sold and the extent to which they were competitive.

Germany—In *Canon Trade Mark Application* [1998] ETMR 77, the Bundesgerichtshof has referred to the ECJ two questions relating to the determination of similarity of goods. First, can one take into account the fame of the earlier trade mark relied upon in opposition to the application when judging the similarity of goods and services? Secondly, can one take into account the fact that the trade recognises that the goods and/or services are of different origin? Advocate-General Jacobs has given his

Opinion on this reference (*Canon Kabushiki Kaisha v. Pathé Communications Corporation* [1998] ETMR 366). He has advised:

(a) Account may be taken of the distinctive character of the mark, in particular the reputation of the earlier mark, in deciding whether there is sufficient similarity to give rise to a likelihood of confusion.

(b) There will only be a likelihood of confusion within the meaning of Article 4(1)(b) if it is likely that the public will be confused into thinking that there is some sort of trade connection between the suppliers of the goods or services in question.

Likelihood of association— At end of p. 169: The decision of Mr Justice Laddie in *Wagamama Limited v. City Centre Restaurants plc* is reported at [1995] F.S.R. 713. His judgment caused some controversy both in rejecting the admissibility of the Statements in the Council Minutes and for finding that "likelihood of association" does not include non-origin confusion. For discussion on this decision, see Anselm Kamperman Sanders, "The *Wagamama* Decision: Back to the Dark Ages of Trade Mark Law" [1996] EIPR 3 and the riposte to this article in Prescott, "Think Before You Waga Finger" [1996] EIPR 317.

It may be that one of Mr Justice Laddie's grounds for rejecting the admissibility of the Statements, namely that they were confidential, has been undermined by their publication in the Official Journal of the Office for Harmonisation of the Internal Market. Thus, the Statements and the corresponding one for the CTM are published in [1995] OJOHIM at 607 and 613 respectively. However, in the United Kingdom, a certified copy of the Minutes will be required for them to be provable in court because of the provisions of the European Communities Act 1972.

In C–251/95 *Sabel v. Puma AG* [1998] ETMR 1; [1998] R.P.C. 199; [1998] 1 C.M.L.R. 445 (ECJ), the Court of Justice was concerned with the interpretation of the words "likelihood of confusion which includes the likelihood of association with the earlier mark" in Article 4(1)(b) of the Directive. A Dutch applicant sought registration in Germany of a mark consisting of a leaping cat device together with the word "Sabel". The application was opposed by the proprietors of two German registered trade marks, each of which featured a leaping cat device. The Bundesgerichtshof referred to the ECJ the issue as to the exact meaning of this phrase and as to whether mere association which the public might make as a result of their analogous semantic content was sufficient for the purpose of Article 4(1)(b). The ECJ said:

"The global appreciation of the visual, aural or conceptual similarity of the marks in question, must be based on the overall impression given by the marks, bearing in mind, in particular, their distinctive and dominant components. The wording of Article 4(1)(b) of the Directive . . . 'there exists a likelihood of confusion on the part of the public' show that the perception of marks in the mind of the average consumer of the type of goods or services in question plays a decisive role in the global appreciation of the likelihood of confusion. The average consumer normally perceives a mark as a whole and does not proceed to analyse its various details.

In that perspective, the more distinctive the earlier mark, the greater will be the likelihood of confusion. It is therefore not impossible that the conceptual similarity resulting from the fact that two marks use images with analogous semantic content may give rise to a likelihood of confusion where the earlier mark has a particularly distinctive character, either *per se* or because of the reputation it enjoys with the public.

However, in circumstances such as those in point in the main proceedings, where the earlier mark is not especially well known to the public and consists of an image with little imaginative content, the mere fact that the two marks are conceptually similar is not sufficient to give rise to a likelihood of confusion."

The Court thus answered the question by saying that "the mere association which the public might make between two trade marks as a result of their analogous semantic content is not in itself a sufficient ground for concluding that there is a likelihood of confusion within the meaning" of Article 4(1)(b). The Court's decision is most welcome in clarifying the meaning of the phrase. However, it is troubling that the Court has permitted the reputation of the mark (*i.e.* how well known the mark is to the public) to become a factor in deciding there is a likelihood of confusion in the classic trade origin sense in Article 4(1)(b). The Directive specifically distinguishes between rights based on registrations and rights based on use of the mark. Rights based on use are considerably curtailed and essentially relate to passing off (or unfair competition) or "well-known" marks within the meaning of Article 6*bis* of the Paris Convention. To blur this distinction is to make the whole process of registration much more uncertain and reliant upon evidence rather than mere examination of advertised marks.

See also the decision of Advocate-General Jacobs in *Sabel v. Puma* reported at [1997] ETMR 283.

For the UK's approach to Article 5(2), see para. 3.071 and the cases cited there.   3.074

(vi) Exhaustion of the rights conferred by a trade mark

In Case C–355/96 *Silhouette International Schmied GmbH & Co v.* 3.075
Hartlauer Handelsgesellschaft mbH [1998] ETMR 286, Advocate-General Jacobs in his opinion recommended that Article 7(1) must be interpreted as meaning that the proprietor of a trade mark can prevent a third party from using the mark for goods which have been put on the market

under that mark outside the EEA. Thus, he advised that there is no discretion for Member States to permit an international exhaustion of rights principle over and above a Community-wide exhaustion of rights principle. The case concerned the importation of out of date SILHOU-ETTE sunglasses put on the market in Bulgaria with the owner of the mark's consent. A parallel importer sought to re-import them back into Austria claiming infringement of trade mark. In his Opinion, he says that Article 7(1) only provides for a Community-wide exhaustion of rights principle. The issue was whether Member States have a discretion to permit an international exhaustion of rights principle. He considered that Article 7(1) did preclude such a discretion. He said that Article 7(1) is a derogation from the rights conferred on the trade mark owner and thus should be construed narrowly. To permit an international exhaustion of rights principle would widen the effect of Article 7(1).

Furthermore, the Advocate-General noted that the directive aims to approximate those national provisions of law which most directly affect the functioning of the common market. He considered that the principle of international exhaustion of rights was central to the functioning of the internal market. In particular, if Member States adopted different stances on its applicability, such would permit imports into one Member State but prevent their export to another Member State.

In doing so, he distinguished *Case E–2/97 Mag Instrument Inc. v. California Trading Company Norway, Ulsteen* [1998] ETMR 85; [1998] 1 C.M.L.R. 331 where the EFTA court interpreted the equivalent provision in relation to the EFTA states and held EFTA states had a discretion to decide whether to introduce or maintain the principle of international exhaustion of rights. He further rejected arguments by the Swedish government that a directive based on Article 100a could not regulate the question of international exhaustion and that it was no part of the essential function of a trade mark to enable the owner to divide up markets. Moreover, he held that the Community Trade Mark did not permit an international exhaustion of rights principle and it would be odd if the directive came to a different result.

On July 16, 1998, the ECJ gave judgment in *Silhouette* and in doing so followed the Advocate-General's Opinion and his reasoning. Thus, it held that national rules providing for exhaustion of trade mark rights in respect of products put on the market outside the EEA under that mark by the proprietor or with its consent are contrary to Article 7(1) of the Trade Mark Directive.

See also Hays & Hansen, *"Silhouette is Not the Proper Case upon which to decide the parallel importation question"* [1998] EIPR 276. In this article, the authors argue that the case is one of re-importation, *i.e.* the goods had previously been put on the market in the EEA. Whilst this may be true, the point is that the ECJ has ruled pursuant to Article 177, *i.e. if the products have been first put on the market outside the EEA.* It is open to the Austrian courts to decide to the contrary. For meaning of "first put on the market", see para. 7.015.

At end of paragraph, add: Advocate-General Jacobs has given his opinion in Case C–427/93, C–429/93 and C–436/93 *Bristol-Myers Squibb v. Paranova* and Cases C–72/94 and C–73/94 *Eurim Pharm v. Beiersdorf* (reported at [1996] F.S.R. 225 and [1996] 5 EIPR D–156) which were cases concerning repackaging of trademarked goods and are similar cases to *Bayer v. Paranova*. In these cases, the questions posed were (1) in what circumstances may a trade mark owner rely on its trade mark to oppose further marketing of repackaged goods? and (2) what sorts of specific rulings could enable the national courts to resolve particular problems that have arisen in some of the "repackaging" cases? Advocate-General Jacobs confirmed the traditional rule prior to the Trade Mark Directive that the proprietor of the mark cannot invoke it in order to prevent such marketing unless the repackaging is done in such a way that it is capable of affecting the original condition of the goods or otherwise impairing the reputation of the trade mark.

The ECJ has now given its decision in these cases (C–232/94, *Bristol-Myers Squibb v. Paranova; Eurim-Pharm v. Beiersdorf; MPA Pharma v. Rhône-Poulenc* [1996] ETMR 1; [1997] F.S.R. 102; [1997] 1 C.M.L.R. 1151. This decision confirms that Article 7 of the Directive and Articles 30 to 36 are to be interpreted in the same way (at para 40). Accordingly, this decision is considered in depth at paras 7.062 and 7.063 below in relation to the interaction of Articles 30 to 36 and trade mark rights in relation to the repackaging of trademarked products as there already exists a substantial corpus of case law in this area.

In C–337/95 *Parfums Christian Dior SA v. Evora BV* [1998] 1 C.M.L.R. 737; [1998] ETMR 26; [1998] R.P.C. 166 (ECJ), the Court of Justice had to consider the effect of Article 7(2) of the Directive. The facts were that the first plaintiff was the owner of various perfume trade marks such as EAU SAVAGE and POISON. The second plaintiff was the sole representative of the first plaintiff in the Netherlands and distributed its branded perfumes through a selective distribution system. The defendant also purchased the plaintiffs' perfumes on the gray market and sold them through its own chain of stores. It also advertised the plaintiff's perfumes for sale. The plaintiffs brought proceedings for trademark and copyright infringement in the Netherlands. The *Hoge Raad* referred to the Court various questions concerning the rights of the parties under the Directive.

The Court held a reseller is free not only to resell goods put on the market with the trademark owner's consent but also to make use of the trade mark in order to bring to the public's attention the further commercialisation of the goods. The Court then went on to consider the effect of Article 7(2). It said that a balance must be struck between the legitimate interests of the trade mark owner in being able to protect the reputation of the mark and the reseller's legitimate interest in being able to sell the goods by using advertising methods customary to its sector of the trade. Where the goods were prestigious and luxury goods, the reseller must endeavour to prevent advertising which affects the value of the trade mark by detracting from the allure and prestigious image of the goods in question and their aura of luxury. Thus, the fact that a reseller uses advertising modes which are customary in his trade sector but not the same as those used by the trade mark owner or his approved retailers is not in itself a legitimate reason within the meaning of Article 7(2) unless it is established that given the specific circumstances of the case, the use of the trade mark in the reseller's advertising "seriously damages the reputation of the trade mark".

See *Phytheron International S.A. v. Jean Bourdoin* Case C–352/95 [1997] F.S.R. 936; [1997] 3 C.M.L.R. 199, where the Court of Justice reaffirmed that it was immaterial in considering the doctrine of exhaustion of rights whether or not the product protected by the mark had been manufactured in a non-member state or not if it had been lawfully first put on the market in the Community. The Court also said that the mere addition of a label onto a product which contained mandatory legislative information could constitute a legitimate reason within Article 7(2) provided it did not omit important information or give inaccurate information and its presentation was not likely to damage the reputation of the trade mark or its owner.

3.077 **The Netherlands**—In *Le Lido SA v. National Stichtung* [1997] ETMR 537, the Court of Appeal and the Court of Cassation of the Netherlands held *sub silentio* that in an application for revocation for non-use of the Dutch mark "LE LIDO" which was resisted by the owner who ran a cabaret and nightclub in the Champs Elysee in Paris, that it was not sufficient to show that Dutch travel agents had merely advertised the Parisian for the owner show in their documentation.

United Kingdom—In *Safeway Stores plc v. Hachette Filipacchi Presse* [1997] ETMR 552, the English High Court held that the use of the word "ELLE" did alter the distinctive character of the mark "elle" (consisting of the word "elle" contained with the female sign ♀) so that it could not be relied upon in defence of an action for revocation of the device mark.

In *Glen Catrine Bonded Warehouse Ltd's Application for Revocation* [1996] ETMR 56, the UK Trade Marks Registry held that United Kingdom legislation which enacted Article 12 of the Directive gave a discretion to the registry not to revoke the trade mark if the grounds for non-use are made out. The Hearing Officer considered that the wording in Article 12 "A trade mark shall be liable for revocation . . . " conferred a discretion on construction of the wording.

3.078 See *Fratelli Graffione v. Ditta Fransa* [1997] ETMR 71; [1997] 1 C.M.L.R. 925, where the ECJ held that Article 12(2)(b) left it to national law to determine whether and to what extent the use of a revoked trade mark must be prohibited. The Italian Corte d'Appello di Milano had declared the trade mark "COTONELLE" for toilet paper void because it misled consumers into believing that the product contained cotton. Furthermore, it injuncted Scott from using the mark because it was a misleading mark. On reference under Article 177, the ECJ held that Article 12(2)(b) of the Trade Mark Directive did not preclude a prohibition as made by the Italian courts. This would seem to be a commonsense decision because clearly the effect of revocation is merely to invalidate the registered mark and thus remove a monopoly and render the mark free for use by everyone. A statutory order prohibiting everyone from using the mark on the grounds of misdescription is prima facie unrelated to the validity of the mark although a mark may become invalid if it is likely to mislead.

(x) Collective marks, guarantee marks and certification marks

In case this was in doubt, the Council and Commission have said that the Directive does not oblige a Member State to introduce service, collective marks and guarantee or certification marks—*Joint Statement by Council and Commission entered in the Minutes of the Council Meeting at which the CTM Regulation was adopted on December 20, 1993 [1996] OJO-HIM 607.* 3.079

(c) Regulation on the protection of geographical indications and designations of origin for agricultural products and foodstuffs

Regulation 2081/92—Commission Regulation 2037/93 lays down detailed procedural rules regarding an application for designation of origin or geographical indication of origin—it is set out in [1996] OJO-HIM 375. Regulation 1107/96 lists those names which would be registered on protected geographical indications or protected designations of origin pursuant to the "fast track" procedure under Article 17 of Council Regulation 2081/92. 3.081

Italy—In *Pilsen Urquell v. Industrie Poretti SpA* [1998] ETMR 168, the Supreme Court of Cassation of Varese, Italy considered the interaction of registered trade marks and geographical indications of origin. It held that geographical place names are "more than capable of being the subject matter of a registered trade mark". The Court was not specifically concerned with the EC Regulation but similar international conventions (Lisbon Agreement for the Protection of Appellations of Origins and their International Registration of October 31, 1958, Stockholm Text of July 14, 1967) which were applicable in Italy. The case concerned the use of the "Pilsener" word for beer. The action was brought by Pilsen Urquell who owned a registered trade mark for Pilsener for beer and a protected geographical indication for the word "Pilsener" as meaning beer coming from the locality of Plzen in the former state of Czechoslovakia. The Defendant had used the word for its beer which was not produced in the Plzen locality but which was brewed in the Pilsener fashion. The Court of first instance held that the word merely meant a method for brewing beer in the eyes of the public and not beer from the Plzen locality. The Supreme Court held that if the term merely meant a method of brewing then both actions would fall away. However, in remitting the matter back to the trial court, it ruled that one should be wary of taking judicial notice of such matters and that registration raises a presumption of validity which the defendant must displace.

England — In *Consorzio del Prosciutto di Parma v. Asda Stores Limited and Hygrade Foods Limited* [1998] 2 C.M.L.R. 215; [1998] E.T.M.R. 481 (English High Court), the Plaintiff sought an injunction to restrain the Defendants from slicing and packaging for sale Parma ham in the UK. The Plaintiff relied on Regulation 2081/92 and Regulation 1107/96 which listed Parma ham amongst those names which were protected designations of origin. There was no issue that the ham came from Parma. The issue was whether the defendants were entitled to slice and package Parma ham or whether this had to be done exclusively in plants approved by the Plaintiff. The judge held that neither regulation referred expressly to slicing and packaging and the fact that the plaintiff's application for registration included such a reference was insufficient to bring it within the Regulations. The judge held that in order for the designation of origin to be protected, Regulation 2081/92 required that the qualities and character of the agricultural products in question be essentially due to the specific geographical location. On the facts, these qualities included the production, processing and preparation of Parma ham, but not the slicing or the packaging. Although not necessary to the decision, the judge further held that if the Regulations were intended to have the effect of regulating slicing and packaging, they could not have direct effect because the provision in question was not clear, precise and unconditional. The application to register was not published in the Official Journal or elsewhere. Consequently, there was no Community source of law from which the Defendants could have learned of the alleged prohibition. The judge further held that the Regulations were intended to be enforceable by private producers but not by trade associations (as the Plaintiff was in this case).

In *Jacques Pistre and ors v. France* [1998] ETMR 457, ECJ, the Court of Justice was concerned with a reference from the French criminal court where proceedings had been brought against individuals who managed salted meat manufacturing companies in the Tarn region of France for applying the word "montagne" and "Monts de Lacaune" to cooked meats without obtaining permission to use such "appellations" as required pursuant to French law. One of the questions referred to the Court was whether French law was compatible with Regulation 2081/92. Article 13(2) of the Regulation only permitted Member States to maintain their own equivalent national measures for a limited transitional period. After such period, protection of "names of origin" and "indications of geographical origin" had to comply with the definitions as laid down in the regulation. The ECJ held that there was no conflict between the French law which required "montagne" to be used only for produce from mountain areas (which was specifically defined) and Regulation 2081/92 because the definition for "montagne" transcended national boundaries and did not denote a specific regional area. Thus, the national law limited itself to giving general protection to a name evoking in consumers qualities abstractly linked to the origin of products from mountain areas. This was held be to too far removed from the material objective of Regulation 2081/92 for it to conflict with it.

6. TABLES

TABLE A—Table of trade mark protection in European countries

Country	Paris Convention	Madrid Agreement[1]	Protocol to Madrid Agreement	E.C. State Trade Mark Directive implemented?
AUSTRIA[5]	●	●	●	●
BELGIUM[5]	●[1]	●	●	●[6]
BULGARIA	●	●	●	
CZECH Republic	●	●	●	
DENMARK[5]	●		●[3]	●[7]
FINLAND[5]	●		●	●
FRANCE[5]	●	●	●	●[8]
GERMANY	●	●	●	●[9]

GREECE[5]	●		●	●[10]
HUNGARY	●	●	●	
IRELAND[5]	●		●	
ITALY[5]	●	●	●	●[13]
LUXEMBOURG[5]	●[1]	●	●	●[6]
MONACO[5]	●	●	●	
NETHERLANDS[5]	●[1]	●	●	●[6]
NORWAY	●		●[3]	
POLAND	●	●	●[3]	
PORTUGAL[5]	●	● (Nice Revision)	●	●[11]
ROMANIA	●	●	●	
RUSSIA	●	●	●	
SLOVAKIA	●	●		
SPAIN[5]	●	●	●	
SWEDEN[5]	●		●[3]	●
UNITED KINGDOM[5]	●		●[3,4]	●[12]
E.C.			●[2]	N/A

NOTES

[1] The territories of these countries are for the application of the Madrid Agreement deemed under Article 9quarter to be one territory.

[2] Accession under Article 14(1)(b) of the Protocol.

[3] Declarations under Article 5(2)(b) and (c) of Protocol permitting national offices a longer time limit for notifying refusals.

[4] Declaration under Article 8(7) of the Protocol allowing national offices to charge international fees equivalent to domestic fees for similar applications.

[5] Member State of the European Community.

[6] Benelux Trade Mark Law 2/12/1992 (not yet in force but expected soon).

[7] Danish Trade Mark Law 341, 6/6/1991.

[8] French Trade Mark Law 92-597 of 1/7/1992 (Intellectual Property Code).

[9] German Trade Mark Law (Markengesetz) 1/1/1995●.

[10] Greek Trade Mark Law, Law No. 2239/1994 (in force from 1st November 1994).

[11] Portuguese Trade Mark Law coming into force on 1st June 1995.

[12] UK Trade Marks Act 1994.

[13] Legislative Decree 480 4/12/1992.

TABLE B—Enactment of optional provisions of Trade Mark Directive by Member States

	3.2(a)	3.2(b)	3.2(c)	3.2(d)	3.3 (2nd sentence)	4.4(a)	4.4(b)	4.4(c)
AUSTRIA		•		•			•	
BELGIUM				•	•	•	•[11]	
DENMARK	•	•	•		•	•	•	•
FINLAND	•[12]	•[12]	•	•	•	•	•	•
FRANCE	•	•	•	•	•	•	•	•
GERMANY	•			•	•[2]	•	•	•
GREECE		•	•	•		•	•	•
IRELAND	•	•	•	•	•	•	•	•
ITALY	•	•	•	•	•	•	•	•
LUXEMBOURG					•	•	•[11]	
MONACO[NK]								
NETHERLANDS					•	•	•[11]	
PORTUGAL	•	•	•	•		•	•[3]	•[4]
SPAIN[NIF]								
SWEDEN		•	•	•	•	•	•	•
UNITED KINGDOM	•		•[5]	•	•	•	•	•

	4.4(d)	4.4(e)	4.4(f)	4.4(g)	4.5	5.2	9.2	
AUSTRIA				●[12]	●			
BELGIUM	●	1	●	6	●	●		
DENMARK	●	●	●		●	●	●[7]	
FINLAND	●	●		●	●	●	●	
FRANCE	●	●		●	●	●		
GERMANY	●	1		●[8]		●	●	
GREECE				●	●	●		
IRELAND					●	●		
ITALY	●	●	●	●		●	●	
LUXEMBOURG	●	1	●	6	●	●		
MONACO								
NETHERLANDS	●	1	●	6	●	●		
PORTUGAL	●	●		●	●	●		
SPAIN								
SWEDEN				●	●	●	●	
UNITED KINGDOM	●		●[9]	●[10]	●	●	●	

NOTES
NK Not Known.
NIF Directive not implemented.
  [1] Country does not provide for certification or guarantee marks.
  [2] Acquired secondary meaning at date of decision upon entry is decisive.
  [3] Prior use of nonregistered mark confers a priority period for a maximum period of six months.
  [4] Firms, company names, business names, shop signs and copyright.
  [5] Royal arms and insignia and national flags are included.
  [6] Benelux laws requires the fulfilment of certain other conditions—see 4.6.b and 14.B of draft Benelux Trade Mark Law.
  [7] No specific clause in Denmark but practice is clear on this point.
  [8] No specific provision but general protection for bad faith applications and also protection under unfair competition laws.

[9] Any trade mark that has expired within a year of the application must be taken into account unless there has been no use of the trade mark for two years prior to its expiry.

[10] General protection for bad faith applications.

[11] Prior users of non-registered marks only given protection if application was made in bad faith.

[12] Protection only if mark protected under Article 6*bis* of Paris Convention.

Chapter Four

COPYRIGHT IN EUROPE

3. European Community Legislation

(a) EEC Green Paper on Copyright

4.021 The Commission has produced a Green Paper which examines a range of issues arising from the impact of the new technologies and the information society on copyright and related issues. The Commission's intention is to reconcile the need for a high level of protection for right holders with the need for free movement of information society services within the Community. The Commission has now proposed a directive in this area—see para 4.083A.

(b) Directive harmonising the term of protection copyright and certain related rights

(x) Date for implementation of directive

4.030 The United Kingdom has introduced the Duration of Copyright and Rights in Performances Regulations 1995 (S.I. 1995 No. 3297), which amend the Copyright, Designs and Patents Act 1988. Where copyright has been "revived", *i.e.* it had expired before the regulation came into effect, the copyright is deemed licensed subject to the payment of a reasonable royalty which is to be set by the Copyright Tribunal if the parties cannot agree.

(c) E.C. Rental and Neighbouring Rights

(i) Introduction

4.031 All countries except Ireland have now implemented the directive. The Commission has brought infringement proceedings against Ireland to implement the directive.

(d) Copyright and Neighbouring Rights relating to satellite and broadcasting

(vii) Implementation of Directive

4.050 The Satellite and Retransmission Directive has now been implemented by all Member States except Greece. The Commission decided to initiate proceedings against Greece for its failure to implement the directive. It is not clear what the outcome of those proceedings have been.

(e) Database Directive

(i) Introduction

The Database Directive has now been adopted (Directive 96/9/E.C. of 4.051 March 11, 1996 [1996] O.J. L77/20). Important amendments were made by the Economic and Social Committee. Accordingly, it differs in some important aspects from the draft commented on in the book. These are considered at the relevant section.

The Database Directive has been implemented in the United Kingdom—The Copyright and Rights in Databases Regulations 1997. It came into force on January 1, 1998. See commentary in *The Copyright and Rights in Databases Regulations 1997: Some Outstanding Issues on Implementation of the Database Directive* [1998] EIPR 178 and *Database Protection in the United Kingdom: The New Deal and its Effect on Software Protection* [1998] EIPR 32.

Belgium, Denmark, Greece, Ireland, Italy, Luxembourg, the Netherlands and Portugal have not implemented the Database Directive (the others have). The Commission has decided to send reasoned opinions to these countries.

(ii) Proposed E.C. Database Directive

(1) Definitions

The definition of "database" in the actual Directive is now: 4.053

> "a collection of independent works, data or other material arranged in a systematic or methodical way and individually accessible by electronic or other means" (Article 1(2)).

This amends considerably the previous definition. The Recitals state that:

> "Whereas the term 'database' should be understood to include literary, artistic, musical or other collections of works or collections of other material such as text, sound, images, numbers, facts and data whereas it should cover collection of independent works, data or other materials which are systematically or methodically arranged and can be individually accessed whereas this means that a recording or an audiovisual, cinematographic, literary or musical work as such does not fall within the scope of this Directive." (Recital 17)
>
> "Whereas as a rule, the compilation of several recordings of musical performances on a CD does not come within the scope of

this Directive, both because, as a compilation, it does not meet the conditions for copyright protection and because it does not represent a substantial enough investment to be eligible under the *sui generis right.*" (Recital 19)

"Whereas the protection provided for in this Directive relates to databases in which works, data or other materials have been arranged systematically or methodically whereas it is not necessary for those materials to have been physically stored in an organised manner." (Recital 21)

"Whereas electronic databases within the meaning of this Directive may also include devices such as CD-ROM and CD-i." (Recital 22)

The definition and the Recitals confirm the following:

(a) Databases which are not computerised, *e.g.* railway timetables, will now be protected. The previous definition only covered electronic databases.

(b) Mere compilations of work is musical compilations which have not involved any effort or investment will not be protected as databases.

(c) Multimedia works will qualify as databases, *e.g.* a multimedia CD-ROM encyclopaedia.

(d) In the case of electronic databases, it is the method of arrangement which is important which must be systematic and not the physical storage of such material.

(e) A random collection of works compiled together will not qualify as a database because such is not systematic or methodical.

(2) Owner of rights in a database

4.054 The definition of "owner of the rights in a database" has been dispensed with. Thankfully, the legislators realised that it was an awkward and complex definition and gave rise to the problems identified in this book. Instead, the Directive distinguishes between the "author of a database" and the "maker of a database". The author of a database is the "natural person or group of persons who created the base or where the legislation of the Member State so permits, the legal person designated as the rightholder by that legislation" (Article 4(1)—this clearly refers to legislation that an employer owns the copyright in an employee's work see; Recital 29). This definition is under the "Copyright" section of the Directive and is clearly only relevant to who owns the copyright in the database (*i.e.* see Article 4(2)) which states that "Where collective works are recognised by the legislation of a Member State, the economic rights shall be owned by the person holding the copyright."

The "maker of the database" is not defined in the Directive or referred to in the Recitals. Instead, the Directive merely provides that the "maker of a database" shall own the *sui generis* right.

It is not clear whether there is any distinction to be made between the "creator of a database" which underpins the definition of the "author of the database" and the "maker of the database". "Maker" suggests something uncreative and functional. "Creator" suggests something creative wherein value is added. This would certainly accord with the differing rights, namely copyright and the *sui generis* right. Still, it is difficult to envisage circumstances where the creator of the database is not the maker. Perhaps, where a company makes arrangements for the surveying of the public and compiling of useful market statistics into a database but entrusts the presentation of such data to a consultant, the latter would be called the creator and the former the maker.

(3) Protection of database by copyright

The reference to Article 2(5) has been removed. Now, the only requirement for a database to be protected by copyright is where databases,

4.055–
4.056

> "by reason of the selection or arrangement of their contents, constitute the author's own intellectual creation" (Article 3(1)).

Thus, a collection of data may now be subject to copyright if it fulfils the definition. No other criteria is relevant for determining the eligibility of a database for copyright protection (Article 3(1)).

The Recitals state that the copyright protection "should cover the structure of the database" (Recital 15). However, it is still provided that no aesthetic or qualitative criteria should be applied in considering the issue of copyright protection (Recital 16).

Thus, one must merely ask the question whether the selection or arrangement of the contents constitutes the author's own intellectual creation. The comments in the penultimate paragraph of section 4.056 still remain.

Interrelationship of copyright in database and copyright in contents—FOOTNOTE 13: Add: The Directive keeps these provisions as Article 3(2) and 7(4)).

4.057

Nonapplicability to non-electronic databases—This provision has not been implemented (see definition of "database", above). See also Recital 14 which specifically states that protection under the Directive extends to cover non-electronic databases. Thus, a railway timetable is capable of being protected under the Directive.

4.058

Definition of "author"—The provisions referred to in this paragraph remain although they are now Article 4(1), (2) and (3).

4.059

(4) Restricted acts regarding copyright in database

4.060   There is now no reference to the owner of the rights in the database having protection only "in respect of the selection or arrangement of the contents of the database". Instead, Article 5 states that:

> "In respect of the expression of the database which is protectable by copyright, the author of a database shall have the exclusive right to carry out or to authorise" [then follows the restricted acts which are almost identical to those provided in the draft at Article 6].

This means that the issue of infringement will be determined according to national law and the gloss provided by the draft will not alter such considerations. However, generally, when considering whether infringement has occurred, consideration is taken of in what way the work is original. Accordingly, in considering the issue of infringement, it is likely that national courts will most likely consider whether the selection or arrangement of the database, which gives it originality, has been copied. If that is so, then the commentary in the book on whether infringement has occurred when a database is merely "downloaded" will still apply.

Article 6 provides that the lawful user of a database will not require the consent of the author of the database where such acts are necessary for the purposes of access to the contents of the database and where such is ancillary to normal use of the contents. Article 6(2) sets out various fair dealing provisions which are discussed below.

(5) Unauthorised extraction right

4.061   The provisions regarding the unauthorised extraction right have been somewhat changed although the essential idea remains. Article 7(1) (the equivalent of Article 10(2)) states that:

> "Member States shall provide for a right for the maker of a database which shows that there has been qualitatively and/or quantitatively a substantial investment in either the obtaining, verification or presentation of the contents to prevent extraction and/or re-utilisation of the whole or a substantial part, evaluated qualitatively and/or quantitatively, of the contents of the database."

This provision makes it clear that not every database will merit the protection of the *sui generis* right. Makers of a database must demonstrate that they have made a substantial investment into making the database. The criteria is purely financial. The right is not based on the work being an original or intellectual creation. Extraction is defined as the permanent or temporary transfer of all or a substantial part of the contents of a database to another medium by any means or in any form. Re-utilisation means any form of making available to the public all, or a substantial part of, the contents of a database by the distribution of copies, by renting, by on-line or other forms of transmission (although the first sale of a copy of a database will exhaust the right to control resale of that copy within the Community)—Article 7(2).

Rights of lawful users

The Directive confirms that a lawful user of the database may extract and/or re-utilise insubstantial parts of its contents (evaluated qualitatively and/or quantitatively) without infringing the *sui generis* right of the maker of the database—Article 8(1). However, he may not perform acts which conflict with the normal exploitation of the database or unreasonably prejudice the legitimate interests of the maker of the database—Article 8(2). These provisions cannot be contracted out of (Article 15). However, such lawful use may not prejudice the holder of copyright or a related right in respect of the works or subject matter contained in the database—Article 8(3).

The Directive retains the provision that the *sui generis* right is independent of the eligibility of the database or its contents for protection by copyright.

The *sui generis* right only applies to databases whose makers or right holders are nationals of a Member State or who have their habitual residence in the territory of the Community or to companies or firms who have their registered office or principal place of business within the Community—Article 11.

Abolition of compulsory licensing provisions

The provisions on compulsory licensing of the unauthorised extraction right contained in the draft are not repeated in the Directive.

(6) Term of protection

The duration of protection under copyright and the *sui generis* right remain as printed although the Directive uses different wording—Article 10. The Directive is silent on the duration of protection under copyright and that will thus be determined according to national laws. In relation to the *sui generis* right, the provisions have been slightly altered. If the database is made available to the public, it is 15 years from the first of January of the year following the date when it was first made available. If it was not made available to the public, protection expires 15 years from the first of January of the year following the date of completion —Article 10.

Moreover, Article 10(3) states that "Any substantial change, evaluated qualitatively or quantitatively, to the contents of a database, including any substantial change resulting from the accumulation of successive additions, deletions or alterations, which would result in the database being considered to be a new investment, evaluated qualitatively and quantitatively, shall qualify the database resulting from that investment for its own term of protection."

4.062

(7) Fair dealing provisions

4.063 There are fair dealing provisions for both the copyright and *sui generis* right in the Directive. However, these differ somewhat from the draft and thus are set out below.

Copyright

Member States may provide that the author of a database cannot prevent the following acts (Article 6(2)):

(a) in the case of reproduction for private purposes of a non-electronic database

(b) where there is use for the sole purpose of illustration for teaching or scientific research, as long as the source is indicated and to the extent justified by the non-commercial purpose to be achieved

(c) where there is use for the purposes of public security or the purposes of an administrative or judicial procedure

(d) where other exceptions to copyright which are traditionally authorised under national law are involved, without prejudice to the above points.

However, the Directive further provides that the above acts may not be applied in a manner which unreasonably prejudices the rightholder's legitimate interests or conflicts with the normal exploitation of the database. The Directive states that repeated and systematic extraction and/or re-utilisation of insubstantial parts of the contents of the database which imply acts which conflict with a normal exploitation of the database or which unreasonably prejudice the legitimate interests of the maker of the database are also not permitted—Article 7(5).

Public lending is deemed not to be an act of extraction or re-utilisation.

Sui generis right

Member States may provide that lawful users of a database may not prevent the following (Article 9):

(a) in the case of extraction for private purposes of the contents of a non-electronic database

(b) in the case of extraction for purposes of illustration for teaching or scientific research, so long as the source is indicated, and to the extent justified by the non-commercial purpose to be achieved

(c) in the case of extraction and/or re-utilisation for the purposes of public security or an administrative or judicial procedure.

(8) Remedies

This provision remains unaltered although reclassified as Article 15.   **4.064**

(9) Transitional provisions

The transitional provisions remain roughly the same although with cer-   **4.065**
tain additions. These are that existing databases already protected by
copyright in a Member State will continue to enjoy protection even if the
effect of the Directive being enacted would be to otherwise remove it
(Article 14(2)). This would have been important to the United Kingdom
where copyright protection applies to compilations including databases
of mundane data in a manner akin to the *sui generis* right but for much
longer period. However, the 1997 Regulations have now specifically
excluded databases from possessing copyright by reason of being a
literary work. Secondly, the Directive makes it clear that the *sui generis*
right will apply to existing databases with the relevant period of protection being taken as 15 years from the first of January following the date
of making (Article 14(3), (5)).

(10) Copyright and extraction right compared

The Directive now makes it abundantly clear that copyright and the *sui*   **4.066**
generis right are entirely independent of each other and independent of
whether or not copyright exists in the contents. There is no repetition of
the third sentence of Article 10(2) (see FOOTNOTE 48 and para. 4.061).
However, advisors should note that the Directive does not permit copyright to exist in collections of data merely because skill and labour have
been involved. It will have to be shown that by reason of the selection or
arrangement of such data, there has been an act of intellectual creation.
That is why there are transitional provisions which permit the continuing
application of copyright to databases in existence already as the Directive
restricts the application of copyright to databases in certain countries,
e.g. the United Kingdom (However, the 1997 Regulations have abolished
copyright in databases by reason of being a literary work save for
databases which were created on or before March 27, 1996—the date of
publication of the directive. Thus, such databases will still be protected
for the remainder of the term of copyright on the basis that such are
literary works).

Insert as new paragraph: **4.066A**

   The Directive requires that Member States bring it into force before
January 1, 1998.

(f) Computer software protection

(iii) Present position in Member States

All European Union Member States have now implemented the Directive   **4.069**
into national law.

4.083A   The Commission has put forward a draft directive for the harmonisation of certain aspects of copyright and related rights in the information
society (*Proposal for a European Parliament and Council Directive on
the harmonisation of certain aspects of copyright and related rights in the
Information Society* Com (97) 628 O.J. 1988 C108/6). The proposal is
somewhat tame (see *The Proposed Directive for Copyright in the Information Society: Nice Rights, Shame about the Exceptions* [1998] EIPR
169). In essence, the aim is to provide copyright protection in an
"on-line" era. Thus, it proposes granting authors the exclusive right to
prohibit the making available to the public of their works in such a way
that members of the public may access them from a place and at a time
individually chosen by them (Article 3). This is aimed at on-line access
where there may be no actual primary or secondary act of infringement
(*i.e.* no temporary reproduction of the protected work). This right is
aimed at all protected works *i.e.* copyright in authored works; performers' rights; phonogram producers rights; film producers rights and broad-
casting and satellite and cable retransmission rights.

There are proposed a number of exceptions which limit the effective-
ness of such exclusive rights. The directive proposes that Member States
provide adequate legal protection against the manufacture and distribution of products which are designed to circumvent copyright-protection
technological measures and the removal of electronic rights-management
information.

4. EEA LEGISLATION

4.084   Bulgaria has acceded to the Rome and Geneva Convention.

CHAPTER FIVE

DESIGN PROTECTION IN EUROPE

3. COMMUNITY LEGISLATION

(a) Green paper on the protection of industrial design

The draft Design Regulation and Directive was considered by the Eco-   5.008
nomic and Social Committee who gave their first opinion on July 6, 1994
([1994] O.J. C388) and an additional opinion on February 22, 1995
([1995] O.J. C110). The European Parliament then discussed the proposal for the Directive (deciding to discuss the Regulation later) and
endorsed the Commission's initiative but subject to 13 amendments.
These amendments concentrated mainly on the definition of design, on
the requirements for protection, the exclusion from protection of certain
elements to promote interoperability of products and, in particular, on
reproduction for repair purposes. The solutions chosen to resolve these
issues will also be of major importance for the future Regulation where
the most material provisions will be essentially identical to those found in
the Directive.

Since then, the Commission has issued an amended proposal for the
Directive which takes into account the vast majority of the amendments
(Amended Proposal for a European Parliament, and Council Directive on
the Legal Protection of Design (COM 99(66))). Subsequently, the Council adopted its common position in accordance with Article 189b of the
Treaty on June 17, 1997 (*Common Position adopted by Council with a
view to adopting Directive 97/ . . . /EC of the European Parliament and
of the Council on the legal protection of designs* [Common Position EC
28/97 O.J. [1997] C237/1). The Common Position differs in only one key
aspect from the Commission's proposal, namely the right of repair. On
October 22, 1997, the European Parliament voted in favour of 12
amendments to the common position in second reading. The Commission has now put forward its opinion (COM (97) 622) on the European
Parliament's amendments to the Council's common position whereby it
accepts some of the amendments proposed but not others.

The main differences between the Council/Commission and Parliament are in relation to (a) abusive disclosures when considering what is
prior art for the purpose of novelty and distinctive character (b) the
"must fit" provision proposed by the Parliament which is wider than that
proposed by the Council and Commission (c) the proposal providing for

mandatory disclosure of counterfeiters which Parliament wishes to keep but the Council and Commission believe does not properly belong in a directive seeking to design substantive design right laws.

On the other hand, the Parliament agrees with the Commission about the need to have a substantive harmonised provision regarding the right to repair whereas the Council does not want immediate harmonisation. Recently, after a marathon conciliation session between the three bodies, it has been agreed to have a "standstill plus", *i.e.* to freeze the existing legislative situation in each Member State in relation to repairs while also allowing any state to liberalise the market further. No obstacle will be allowed to the free movement of the parts in question.

The draft directive must now go through the Article 189(b) hoops again (*i.e.* Commission putting forward a new draft directive; Council adopting a Common Position and Parliament voting on it). It remains to be seen whether the final hurdles can be overcome.

In the rest of this update, one will look at the draft directive as it now stands and highlight the remaining contentious issues over which agreement is proving difficult. As the book has largely concentrated on the proposed Community Design where the substantive proposals in relation to industrial designs are identical, the proposed amendments to the directive will be discussed in relation to what are likely to be identical parallel provisions in any Community Design Regulation.

(i) Proposed community design regulation

5.010 *Definition of design*—The new proposed definition for design is that "design" means "the appearance of the whole or a part of a product resulting from the feature of, in particular, the lines, contours, colours, shape, texture and/or materials of the product itself and/or its ornamentation" (Article 1(a)). The initial proposal by the Parliament that only outwardly visible features be protected has now been dropped because it was intended that the inside of a container be protectable by design right. However, Recital 11 of the common position indicates the need for features for which design protection is sought to be shown visibly in the application for protection. The Council, Commission and Parliament are now aligned on this point.

The protection requirements for a design is that a design is protected by a design right to the extent that it is new and has individual character (Article 3(2)).

Complex products

A complex product is defined as a product which is composed of multiple components which can be replaced permitting disassembly and reassembly of the product (Article 1(c)). A design applied to or incorporated in a product which constitutes a component part of a complex product is only to be considered new and to have individual character:

(a) if the component part, once it has been incorporated into the complex product remains visible during normal use of the latter

(b) to the extent that those visible features of the component part fulfil in themselves the requirements as to novelty and individual character (Article 3(3)(b)).

These amendments make it clear that in a complex product, one can obtain protection for component parts but they must be visible during normal use of the latter. "Normal use" is defined as meaning "use by the end user excluding maintenance, servicing or repair work" (Article 3(4)—*Amendment proposed by Parliament and accepted by Commission in its Opinion*). Thus, this would preclude design protection for parts under a car bonnet e.g. oil filters, fan belts or other engine parts (see also commentary on Common Position by Single Market Commissioner Mario Monti—available on DGXV Web Site). Visible parts like steering wheels or car chairs will qualify for protection being visible parts, however the relatively high threshold for the protection of designs ("novelty" and "individual character") may prevent such qualifying for protection.

The Commission and Parliament are now aligned. It is not thought that this provision will cause a problem with the Council.

Article 9(1) of the original proposal has now been somewhat amended   5.011
(see new Article 7(1)) so that a design right shall not subsist in "features of appearance of a product which are solely dictated by its technical function". This wording is a considerable improvement on the original. Parliament, the Council and the Commission are agreed on this wording. However, there still remains the issue of whether or not this is an objective or subjective test. If the designer set out to produce a purely functional product, does it matter whether or not there are many other designs which look different but perform an identical function?

The definition of "novelty" remains the same as set out in the book.   5.012

The definition of "individual character" is now amended so that the word "significantly" has been dropped following a proposal by Parliament. The Commission considered that this does not unduly lower the threshold because the provision still contains the requirement of a different overall impression. Accordingly, Article 5 now reads:

1. A design shall be considered to have individual character if the overall impression it produced on the informed user differs from the overall impression produced on such a user by any design which has been made available in the public before the date of filing of the application for registration or, if priority is claimed, the date of priority.

2. In assessing individual character, the degree of freedom of the designer in developing the design shall be taken into consideration.

67

Recital 13 (including the proposed amendment by the European Parliament) states that the assessment as to whether a design has individual character is whether the overall impression produced on the informed user viewing the design differs from existing "design corpus" taking into consideration the nature of the products to which the design is applied or in which it is incorporated and in particular the industrial sector to which it belongs and the degree of freedom of the designer in developing the design. The guideline given in the original proposal about the assessment of individual character (Article 6(3) in the original proposal) has been somewhat changed so that it is now only "the degree of freedom of the designer in developing the design" which is important (Article 6(2) in the amended proposal). Accordingly, no weight is now given to common features (as opposed to differences) in considering whether a design has "individual character".

The Commission, Council and Parliament are aligned on the above definitions and recital.

Prior Art—For the purpose of assessing individual character and novelty, Article 6 deems a design to have been made available to the public if it has been published following registration or exhibited, used in trade or otherwise disclosed "except where these events could not reasonably have become known in the normal course of business to the circles specialised in the sector concerned, operating within the Community" before the filing or priority date (Article 6(1)). Thus, the original requirement that the design is commercialised has been dropped. Disclosures by the designer during the 12 month period prior to date of filing or priority are deemed not to be disclosures (Article 6(2)). The Commission, Council and Parliament are in agreement on this. However, there remains a dispute on the effect on registrability of an abusive disclosure in relation to the designer or his successor in title (Article 6(3)—the Commission and Council favour the position that such a disclosure has no effect on the registrability whereas Parliament considers that it is prejudicial if it leads to a registered Community Design or registered design right in the Member State concerned).

5.013   *Exclusive rights*—The amended proposal has introduced a negative definition of the exclusive rights so that "the scope of the protection conferred by a design right shall include any design which does not produce on the informed user a different overall impression" (Article 9(1)). This change is not intended to be of substance but to ensure compatibility between the formulation of the scope of protection and the definition of "individual character". As the Commission says, this avoids a situation whereby a grey area arises when a design is eligible for protection in its own right but constitutes an infringement of a prior design. Consequently, all designs which do not qualify for individual character because a "close" design is protected will be considered to be infringing that "close" design. As with the assessment of "individual character", the Commission has amended the provision whereby in the assessment of the scope of protection, common features are given more weight than differences so that only the degree of freedom of the designer in developing his design is relevant.

The Commission, Council and Parliament are agreed on these provisions.

Article 9(b) in the original proposal is now Article 7(2) in the amended proposal. This has been reworded somewhat because of the wishes of the European Parliament who sought a clearer definition of the "must fit" clause. The current text is closely modelled upon the corresponding provisions of the United Kingdom Copyright, Designs and Patents Act 1988. It now reads that   **5.017**

> "A design right shall not subsist in features of appearance of a product which must necessarily be reproduced in their exact form and dimensions in order to permit the product in which the design is incorporated or to which it is applied to be mechanically connected or placed in, around or against another product so that either product may perform its function."

Unfortunately, the Parliament has now proposed a rather wider drafted "must fit" exception than that set out above. The Commission has stated that it cannot accept this.

The "Lego" defence still remains unchanged (although it is now Article 7(3)).

In relation to the repair provisions, the Commission and Parliament are deadlocked with the Council over the need for a repair derogation. The Commission and Parliament are in favour of a repair clause. The Commission and Parliament propose a remuneration system that will operate as from the date of registration of the design has been introduced. Thus, they propose that in order to be able to make use of the right to repair, the manufacturer or importer of a component part from outside the E.C. to be used in repair must: (i) notify the rightholder of the intended use of the design (ii) offer him a fair and reasonable remuneration and (iii) offer to provide the rightholder with the information in a regular and reliable manner which is needed to establish the correctness of the remuneration paid by the third party. Abuse of the provisions will remove the right to repair (Article 14(4)). In calculating the remuneration, the investment made in the relevant design development shall be the primary basis for consideration (Article 14(3)).   **5.018**

On the other hand, the Council merely proposes a provision whereby Member States may maintain national provisions regarding the permitting of repair of a complex product until amendments (if any) are adopted by the Commission after the first five years of the directive being in force.

Very recently, Parliament and Council managed, at the end of a marathon sitting on the night of Wednesday June 24, to reach agreement under the conciliation procedure. The compromise reached means that the Council has abandoned its position of seeking to allow a "free-for-all", *i.e.* allowing the Member States carte blanche to introduce or change national legal provisions in this area. Parliament made concessions on its preference for a totally harmonised system of fair and reasonable remuneration for right holders for any use of the design of a component part which is used in the repair of a complex product. All are now agreed to have a "standstill plus" provision, *i.e.* to freeze the existing legislative situation in each Member State in relation to repairs while also allowing any state to liberalise the market further. No obstacle will be allowed to the free movement of the parts in question.

5.018A   Insert as new paragraph:

Mandatory disclosure—Parliament has now insisted on an anti-counterfeiting provision being inserted whereby a court having jurisdiction for hearing an action for infringement of design right shall order at the request of the rightholder a person to supply the holder with information as to the origin and the route of commercial distribution of goods allegedly infringing the design right (Article 16(a)). This provision was added in order to provide a means to fight counterfeiting and is closely modelled on German law. United Kingdom practitioners will be familiar with such a provision as often in interlocutory and final actions concerning infringement, the defendant will be required to swear an affidavit giving the names and addresses of those to whom and those from whom infringing products have been supplied.

However, the Council and Commission, although sympathetic to this provision, are now opposed to it because they consider that the directive should not be burdened with this type of procedural provision. The Commission has said that it is better to deal with the issue of counterfeiting in a set of complete measures against counterfeiting. At present, the Commission and Council are thus aligned against the Parliament on this point.

5.020   The relationship between copyright and the proposed design right has been simplified in the latest proposals. Article 18 is now Article 17 in the amended proposal. Article 17 simplifies the rather complex provisions of the old Article 18 and now merely permits cumulative protection under copyright and design rights. Thus, whether a design is also subject to copyright is proposed to be a matter of national law. The originally proposed Article 18(2) (see FOOTNOTE 76 and surrounding text in book) has been deleted. The Commission, Council and Parliament are aligned on this point.

At present, it is proposed that Member States implement the directive three years from the date of its publication in the Official Journal. At present, this seems a long way in the future.

Chapter Six

PLANT VARIETY RIGHTS IN EUROPE

3. Community Regulation on Plant Variety Rights

The Commission has now issued a Regulation establishing implementing   6.019
rules and fees applicable to the CPVR. See Regulation 1238/95 (fees),
Regulation 1239/95 (procedural rules) and Regulation 448/96 which
amends 1239/95. These are all published in the Official Journal of the
Office for Harmonisation of the Internal Market No. 5 of 96.

4. Table of European Countries Who are Members of UPOV

Portugal had deposited its instrument of accession to UPOV.   6.046
   The 1991 UPOV Convention has now been ratified by Denmark, The
Netherlands and Israel. Two more states are required to ratify before it
comes into force.

Chapter Seven

ENFORCEMENT OF INTELLECTUAL PROPERTY

3. Articles 30 to 36: Intellectual Property Doctrines

(g) Differing protection in Member States

7.014   In an interesting development, the High Court of England in *Merck & Co. Inc. v. Primecrown Limited* [1995] F.S.R. 909, has referred a series of questions to the ECJ which inter alia asked whether the rule in *Merck v. Stephar* should be altered. The case was concerned with whether the importation into the United Kingdom of pharmaceutical products marketed in Spain and Portugal by the patentee or with his consent could be prevented by the patentee. Although patent protection for pharmaceuticals is now available in those countries, it was not then, and the transitional provisions preventing the application of the *Merck v. Stephar* principle were due to expire shortly. As there were no retrospective measures, a patentee who had commercialised his product prior to the law permitting the patenting of pharmaceuticals would never have been able to obtain a patent in Spain and Portugal.

Jacob J. noted that at the time of *Merck v. Stephar*, prices for drugs in France and Germany were comparable to those in Italy. Whereas, the price difference between drugs marketed in Spain and those marketed elsewhere are very significant because of governmental price regulation in the Iberian peninsula. Accordingly, the plaintiff submitted that the *Merck v. Stephar* principle would result in massive parallel importing and a distortion of the free market (as indeed had already been recognised by the Head of Directorate-General III). The plaintiff submitted that it would be many years before the unevenness smoothed itself out. Accordingly, Jacob submitted for decision by the ECJ a reference under Article 177 whether the rule still applied in particular if:

(a) the proprietor has and continues to have a legal and/or ethical obligation to market and to continue marketing the pharmaceutical in that country and/or

(b) that country and/or E.C. legislation effectively requires the proprietor once the pharmaceutical is put on the market in that country to supply and continue to supply sufficient quantities to satisfy the needs of domestic patients and/or

(c) that country's legislation grants to its authorities and its authorities exercise the right to fix the sale price of the pharmaceutical in that country and legislation prohibits the sale of the pharmaceutical at any other price and/or

(d) the price of the pharmaceutical in that country has been fixed by its authorities at a level at which substantial exports of the pharmaceutical from such country to the Member State are anticipated with the result that the economic value of the patent would be significantly eroded and the research and development of future pharmaceuticals planned by the proprietor would be significantly undermined contrary to the rationale underlying the recent introduction by the E.C. Council of the Supplementary Protection Certificate.

The case has now been heard by the ECJ (Case C267–268/95 *Merck v. Primecrown Limited* [1997] 1 C.M.L.R. 83). The Court considered the application of *Merck v. Stephar* in circumstances where the patentee claimed that he was under a legal or ethical obligation to provide the drugs in the country where there was no patent protection so that it could not be said that he genuinely consented to the marketing of the drug in the country. The ECJ affirmed the general principle of *Merck v. Stephar*. Thus, a patentee had to accept the consequences of marketing a product on the market in a Member State where the product was not patentable. It said that the argument that low prices imposed by Spain and Portugal reduced the patentee's right to decide freely on the conditions in which they would market their products could not justify a derogation from the principle of the free movement of goods. Distortions caused by different price legislation in a Member State had to be remedied by measures taken by the Community authorities.

However, the ECJ said (in not following the Advocate-General's Opinion) that *Merck v. Stephar* would only not apply where, once the product had been placed on the market in a member state, the patentee was legally obliged to supply and continue to supply sufficient quantities to satisfy the needs of domestic patients. In such circumstances, the patentee could not be deemed to have given his consent to the sale of the product. However, there had to be a genuine existing obligation and the patentee had to prove it (which it failed to do in this case). On the other hand, an alleged ethical obligation to provide supplies of drugs was not a basis for derogating from the rule in *Merck v. Stephar*.

See also further discussion of this case at para 7.016 and 7.017 where Advocate-General Fennelly's Opinion that *Merck v. Stephar* be overturned is discussed.

(h) "Placed on the market"

In *Music Machine, Discover Enterprise and TWS v. IFPI Belgium* [1996]   7.015
1 EIPR D–8, a case involving parallel imports, the issue of what is meant

73

by "first sale in the European Union" was considered by a Belgian court in a case whereby goods were sold from the European Union but delivered outside the European Union. The plaintiff argued that if the place where the phonogram producer has given his consent for the actual sale is in the European Union, then the first sale has occurred within the European Union and an owner of rights in such goods has exhausted his rights. The defendants argued that the concept of first sale should be interpreted as meaning "first making available to the public" with the consent of the rights owner. The Tribunal de Commerce at Brussels held that first sale meant the activity whereby the products are lawfully marketed in one or more Member States of the E.U. This concept had to be assessed taking into account the reasoning behind the protection of phonograph producers' neighbouring rights (the rights in issue). Phonograph producers were granted protection under the new Belgium Act since they were the necessary economic channel through which the works of authors, artists and performers were made available to the public. Consequently, "first sale" did not refer to a sales contract or where the phonogram producer gave his consent but where the product was actually marketed.

See also "Silhouette is not the Proper Case upon which to decide the Parallel Importation Question" *Hays and Hansen* [1998] EIPR 277 where the authors examine the meaning of "first put on the market".

7.016 See discussion of *Pharmon v. Hoechst* in Case C267–268/95 *Merck v. Primecrown Limited* [1997] 1 C.M.L.R. 83 where the ECJ stated that both cases were consistent with the issue as to whether or not the patentee had consented to the marketing of the product in question within the Community.

7.017 In his Opinion in *Merck v. Primecrown*, Advocate-General Fennelly advised the court that they should depart from the principle laid down in *Merck v. Stephar*. The Advocate-General advised that the judgment of *Merck v. Stephar* represented an unacceptable restriction on the proper exercise of national patent rights as in effect, it deprived the patentee of any reward in relation to the marketing of a protected product. Furthermore, he considered the *Musik-Vertrieb Membran* and the *Pharmon v. Hoechst* decisions. He advised that while the decisions could be reconciled on a purely formal level (*i.e.* by reference to the voluntary nature of the licence in *Musik-Vertrieb Membran* and the compulsory nature of the licence in *Pharmon v. Hoechst*), they are incompatible in substance. In echoing the arguments in the book at para 7.014 and 7.017, he pointed out the commercial absurdity of applying too literal a test to the issue of consent by pointing out that in *Musik-Vertrieb Membran* (discussed in para 7.014), if the copyright owner had refused to grant a licence, the record manufacturer could have simply invoked the statutory licence legislation. Thus, he said that it is not easy to differentiate a patentee's avoidance of the inevitable through agreeing contractual terms with a compulsory licence as in *Pharmon v. Hoechst*. He thus advised that a formalist approach to the application of the consent test led to erratic results and focus should be placed on the exhaustion of the "economic substance of the exclusive rights" (citing *Demaret* "Industrial Property Rights, Compulsory Licences and the Free Movement of Goods under Community Law" (1987) Vol. 18 No.2 IIC 161). Later on, in his Opinion, the Advocate-General endorsed Professor Joliet's approach that the exhaustion doctrine is based on the availability of parallel prerogatives in both the country of exportation and that of importation and that a decision applying the doctrine in the absence of such parallelism would be tantamount to lowering the protection available in the country of importation to the level of the less protective legislation of the country of exportation. Thus, he considered that there was no good reason why the previous Spanish and Portuguese policy of refusing to recognise the patentability of pharmaceutical products should have been imposed upon other Member States who abandoned that policy many years before (para 135 of his Opinion).

However, as seen in para 7.014, the ECJ did not follow the Advocate-General's Opinion and upheld the doctrine of *Merck v. Stephar* thus applying their imprimatur to a formalistic approach to the issue of consent. The Court emphasised that in striking the balance between free movement of goods in the Community and the principle of protection of patentees' rights, the right to oppose importation of a product may be exhausted by its marketing in a Member State where it is not patentable (para 37).

(n) International or E.C.-wide exhaustion of rights principle?

7.029 In relation to trade marks, Advocate-General Jacobs in his Opinion in Case C–355/96 *Silhouette International Schmied GmbH & Co v. Hartlauer Handelgesellschaft mbH* [1998] ETMR 286, has held that an international exhaustion of rights principle in relation to trade marks is no longer compatible with Community law. The ECJ has followed that opinion in its judgment dated July 16, 1998. See para 3.075 in the book and this supplement.

4. ANCILLARY DOCTRINES DEVELOPED IN RELATION TO ARTICLE 36

(e) Transitional provisions for acceding States

7.039 At end of paragraph, add: In *Merck & Co. Inc. v. Primecrown Limited* [1995] F.S.R. 909 (discussed above at paras 7.014 to 7.017), Jacob J. referred to the ECJ an issue concerning Article 47 of the Spanish Act of Accession. This provided that patent rights in other Member States could be relied upon to prevent pharmaceutical products marketed in Spain until the end of the third year after Spain had made that product patentable. There was a dispute as to what date this meant. In Spain, one could obtain patent protection for pharmaceuticals as of October 7, 1992. The choice was of five dates: (1) October 7, 1995 (2) December 31, 1995 (3) October 7, 1996 (4) December 31, 1996 (5) the end of the third year after the particular drug became patentable.

The ECJ has now given its ruling in this case. In *Merck v. Primecrown Ltd* Cases C–267/95 and C–268/95 [1997] F.S.R. 237; [1997] I C.M.L.R. 83, the ECJ held that the transitional provisions should be interpreted so as to ensure the earliest application of the free movement of goods, being exactly three years after pharmaceutical products became patentable. Thus, the transitional periods expired on October 6, 1995 for Spain and December 31, 1994 for Portugal.

5. INDIVIDUAL TYPES OF INTELLECTUAL PROPERTY

(a) Trade marks

(x) How much can you interfere with a trade mark if you are a parallel importer?

7.062   In *Bristol-Myers Squibb v. Paranova; Eurim-Pharm v. Beiersdorf; MPA Pharma v. Rhône-Poulenc* [1996] ETMR 1, [1997] F.S.R. 102 [1997] I C.M.L.R. 1151; [1997] I C.M.L.R. 1222 the ECJ revisited the problem of repackaging in the post-Trade Mark Directive era. The Court held that trade marks are an essential element in a system of undistorted competition because they enable consumers to identify products. It held that the owner is entitled to prevent the marketing of its products if their quality or condition has been put at risk by the actions of an importer. The owner is also entitled to prevent the marketing of the repackaged products unless their repackaging was necessary for them to comply with rules in the country of importation.

As previously stated in *Hoffmann-La Roche v. Centrafarm* (No. 2/77) [1978] E.C.R. 1139, [1978] 3 C.M.L.R. 217, the Court reiterated that the owner was not justified in exercising his rights if such amounted to a disguised restriction on trade or the artificial partitioning of the markets. Importantly, the Court held that the importer was not required to demonstrate that the owner had deliberately sought to partition the markets for him to rely on this principle. What mattered was the effect of the owner's exercise not his intentions. Re-emphasising the principles set out in *Hoffmann-La Roche*, the Court said that the importer must comply with the following requirements:

(a) The repackaged product must make it clear who repackaged it

(b) The repackaged product must make it clear who manufactured it

(c) The repackaged product is appropriately presented to the consumer

(d) The importer must give advance notice of the repackaging of the product and supply the owner with a specimen of the repackaged product if so requested.

However, it was not necessary for the repackaged product to state that the repackaging had been carried out without the owner's authorisation.

In Case C–349/95 *Frits Loendersloot v. George Ballantine* [1998] ETMR 10; [1998] 1 C.M.L.R. 993 (E.C.J.), a parallel importer sought to remove identification numbers of Scotch whisky which were used for the purpose of identifying parallel imports and then re-affixed labels which were similar in nature. The ECJ reaffirmed the principles set out in *Hoffmann-La Roche v. Centrafarm* (see para. 7.064 of book) and said that it was for the international court to assess whether those conditions had been satisfied. In particular, the national court should ascertain whether the identification system was meant to hinder parallel imports or comply with national or Community legislation.

(3) Pfizer Inc. v. Eurim-Pharm GmbH

Comment—The recent decision of *Bristol-Myers Squibb v. Paranova*;   7.068
Eurim-Pharm v. Beiersdorf; *MPA Pharma v. Rhone-Poulenc* [1996]
ETMR 1, [1997] F.S.R. 102 [1997] I C.M.L.R. 1151 (discussed in para.
7.062) means that Advocate-General Capotorti's Opinion that the artificial partitioning of the market need not be intended for the practice to fall within Article 6(2) is now the legal position and the Bundesgerichtshof decision in *Hoffmann-La Roche v. Centrafarm* (No. 102/77) must be considered bad law.

(b) Patents

See *BV v. Smith Kline & French Laboratories* [1997] R.P.C. 801; [1998]   7.072
1 C.M.L.R. 1 where the ECJ upheld the right of the patentee to prevent unauthorised manufacture during the life of the patent even where only a few products were made for the purpose of obtaining marketing authorisation once the patent had expired (discussed in detail below at para. 7.079A).

(iii) Differences in Member States' patent laws

In *Smith Kline and French Laboratories Ltd v. Generics BV* [1996] 1   7.073
EIPR D–20, Supreme Court of The Netherlands, Generics submitted the drug cimetidine to the Register of Pharmaceutical Products for the purpose of obtaining regulatory approval whilst the patent for cimetidine which was owned by Smith Kline French was still in force. SKF issued proceedings for patent infringement claiming that submission to the

Register of a patented drug did not fall within the fair dealing provisions of the Dutch Patents Act 1910. As the registration process took approximately 14 months, it sought an injunction preventing Generics from marketing the drug until 14 months after the expiry of the patent. These were granted. On appeal, Generics argued that such a provision and the injunction granted thereon was contrary to Articles 30 to 36 as it constituted a quantitative restriction within Article 30. The Supreme Court has now referred these matters to the ECJ.

The ECJ has now held in *Generics BV v. Smith Kline & French Laboratories Ltd* [1997] R.P.C. 801; [1998] 1 C.M.L.R. 1 that the use of samples made in accordance with a patented process for a medicinal product for the purpose of obtaining a marketing authorisation without the consent of the patentee fell within the specific subject matter of the patent right. There was nothing to suggest that the Netherlands law was discriminatory in nature or that it sought to favour domestic products over those from other Member States. Accordingly, the patentee was justified under Article 36 in obtaining the relief sought. Furthermore, such relief (*i.e.* an injunction) could not of itself be held to be a disproportionate form of reparation.

7.093 In Case C267–268/95 *Merck v. Primecrown Limited* [1997] 1 C.M.L.R. 83, the Court and Advocate-General Fenelly revisited the case of *Warner Bros v. Christiansen* in considering the validity of the decision in *Merck v. Stephar* discussed above at paras 7.016 and 7.017. The Advocate-General was of the opinion that the rationale of *Warner Bros v. Christiansen* was that the exhaustion of one right in one Member State did not exhaust a different right in the same product in another Member State. He advised that *a fortiori* the sale in one Member State without any patent protection should not be taken to exhaust that right in another Member State where such protection exists. Thus, he held that if one applied the statement of the ECJ in *Warner Bros* that "It cannot therefore be accepted that marketing by a film-maker of a video cassette containing one of his works in a Member State which does not provide specific protection for the right to hire out, should have repercussions on the right conferred on that same film maker by the legislation of another Member State to restrain, in that State, the hiring out of that video cassette" to the facts of *Merck v. Stephar*, the conclusion was that the patentee should not have to bear the consequences of marketing in a Member State where its patent right is not recognised (para 134 of his Opinion).

It is submitted that whilst the arguments of the Advocate-General are persuasive, it is wrong to equate the case of *Warner Bros v. Christiansen* with *Merck v. Stephar*. As stated in the book, the nature of a rental right is very different to that of a reproduction right because one copy of a video can be hired out many times and that it would have been manifestly wrong to have ruled that the rental right was exhausted once a copy of a video had been put into circulation as such would render the exclusive right to render wholly useless. In other words, *Warner Bros v. Christiansen* was primarily concerned with the distinction between these two rights and not the fact that a rental right existed in Denmark but not (at the time) in the United Kingdom. Looked at another way, if the video had been put into circulation in Denmark, it would still not have exhausted the rental right in Denmark. Therefore, *a fortiori*, its marketing in the United Kingdom could hardly be more detrimental to the ability to exercise the rental right in Denmark than if it had been first marketed in Denmark.

For an example of a measure which discriminated against foreign produce, see *Jacques Pistre and ors v. France* [1997] ETMR 457, where the ECJ held that the reservation of the appellation "montagne" to only those products produced on home territory and developed from home-produced raw materials meant that the French law discriminated against foreign products made in mountain areas. Accordingly, such a national law could only be justified where appropriate by Article 36. As "montagne" was not an indication of origin, Article 37 could not be invoked. 7.098

CHAPTER EIGHT

LICENSING OF INTELLECTUAL PROPERTY

4. COMMUNITY LAW AND INTELLECTUAL PROPERTY LICENCES

(b) Court and Commission's approach to Article 85(1)

8.026 The Commission has issued a Green Paper on Vertical Restraints in E.C. Competition Policy [1997] 4 C.M.L.R. 519 which is the result of a detailed investigation into the competitive effects of vertical restraints in distribution and franchising arrangements. It has proposed four options —maintaining the current system; providing for wider block exemptions; providing more focussed block exemptions and providing block exemptions with guidelines as compatibility of agreements with Article 85(1) (*i.e.* for instance by providing a rebuttable presumption that a vertical agreement between parties with less than 20 per cent market share is compatible with Article 85(1)). The paper is not specifically aimed at intellectual property licences but it is clear that as such licences are of a vertical nature, it is of interest.

(i) Agreement, decisions and concerted practices

8.030 At end of section, add: See also T–30/91, *Solvay SA v. E.C. Commission* [1996] 5 C.M.L.R. 57 where the CFI held that a concerted practice is characterised by the fact that it substitutes for the risks of competition cooperation between undertakings which lessens each undertaking's uncertainty as to the future attitude of its competitors. If that uncertainty is not lessened, there is no concerted practice. However, parallel conduct is not itself proof of concertation unless concertation constitutes the only plausible explanation of such conduct. Where the Commission alleges parallel conduct, it is necessary to ascertain whether that conduct, taking account of the nature of the products, the site and the number of the undertakings and the volume of the market in question, be explained otherwise than by concertation.

(ii) Undertakings

8.032 In T–77/92, *Parker Pen Limited v. E.C. Commission* [1995] 5 C.M.L.R. 435, the CFI confirmed that the conduct of a company must be regarded as attributable to its parent company where it is a wholly-owned subsidiary of the latter.

The Commission has issued a new Notice on agreements of minor importance which it considers do not fall within Article 85(1) — *Agreements of Minor Importance Notice 1997* [1997] O.J. C372/3; [1998] 4 C.M.L.R. 192. The structure is similar to previous notices. The following are the main changes: **8.038**

(a) Agreements between undertakings with less than 5 per cent aggregate market share threshold where the agreement is a horizontal agreement are considered outside Article 85(1)

(b) Agreements between undertakings with less than 10 per cent aggregate market share threshold where the agreement is at a vertical level are considered outside Article 85(1)

(c) Agreements which contain blatant anti-competitive practices (*i.e.* price fixing; resale price maintenance; market sharing etc.) will not benefit from the above presumptions

(d) Agreements between small and medium-sized undertakings as defined in the Annex to the Commission Recommendation 96/280 [1997] 4 C.M.L.R. 510 will rarely be capable of affecting trade significantly between Member States.

(f) Specific types of intellectual property licence

(v) Plant breeders' rights

For an example of the Commission's generally favourable approach to plant variety licensing where restrictions in the licence are imposed in order to maintain the variety, see *Re the Application of CBA* [1995] 5 C.M.L.R. 730. In that case, the Commission was favourable to (i) licences whereby the licensee undertook to produce the plants exclusively on his own holding for the purpose of his own flower production and that he would obtain propagating material only from the CBA (Chrysanthemum Breeding Association) or other licensees and (ii) licences where the licensee undertook to produce the plants on his own holding and sell propagating material to other licensees and to final consumers/flower growers. Where such material was sold to the latter, the licensee was obliged to impose conditions on such persons whereby the final consumer/flower grower could only use the material exclusively for his own production, did not multiply or market propagating material and could only obtain propagating material from licensees.   **8.095**

In *SICASOV* [1995] 5 C.M.L.R. 100, the Commission took a favourable stance on standard agreements which SICASOV, the French plant variety rights collecting society, proposed to enter into with multipliers wishing to produce and sell seed protected by plant breeders' rights. The relevant clauses contained in the Agreement were:

(a) the production and reproduction licence for the variety is granted solely for the production and sale of seed within French territory or within another patented territory providing for such protection

(b) the licensee may neither export nor import basic seed (of the variety in question) without express approval from SICASOV

(c) a licensee selling basic seed must obtain a commitment from the purchaser that the seed will not be exported either directly or indirectly

(d) the licensee may not export certified seed directly (or through an undertaking belonging to the same group or subject to the same export prohibition) if the variety has been entered into the common catalogue for less than four years

(e) the licensee may not export first- or second-generation certified seed if such seed does not correspond to the lowest degree of certification provided for in the country of destination. The licensee undertakes to impose this obligation on all purchasers. However, the licensee may export certified seed of the generation corresponding to the lowest degree of certification authorised by the country of destination. The breeder accordingly undertakes to give his agreement as a matter of course to the reclassification of seed by the national certification authorities, provided that the exporter informs him of his intention and that the certification authorities inform him (or his assignee) of the quantities of seed reclassified and the country of destination. Such systematic authorisation is to be granted only for varieties entered into the common catalogue for more than four years

(f) the licensee may not export certified seed to Member States which do not grant legal protection for new plant varieties. The licensee undertakes to impose this obligation on all his purchasers

(g) the licensee may not export certified seed to countries which are not Member States or members of the International Union for the Protection of New Varieties of Plants (UPOV). The licensee undertakes to impose this obligation on all his purchasers.

(g) Specific clauses in intellectual property licences

(iii) Export and direct sales bans

8.123   In T–77/92, *Parker Pen Ltd v. E.C. Commission* [1995] 5 C.M.L.R. 3435, the CFI again asserted that an export ban infringed Article 85(1) by its very nature. However, it must still be shown that the ban will have an appreciable effect on trade between Member States. An argument in that case that the export ban had not been implemented was unsuccessful because its existence may create a visual and psychological effect which contributes to the partitioning of the market.

(l) Technology Transfer Block Exemption

(i) Overview

Insert as new paragraph: The Technology Transfer Block Exemption has   **8.261A**
now been adopted [1996] O.J. L1/2 [1996] Antitrust C.M.L.R. 405
[1996] F.S.R. 397. It differs in certain key respects from the draft commented on in the book.

The key difference is that the provision in the draft that the 40 per cent
and 10 per cent ceiling on market share beyond which the Block Exemption was inapplicable has been removed as a result of intense lobbying by
industry. Instead, a much watered-down version of this provision
remains, namely that the Commission may remove the protection conferred by the Block Exemption where there is no effective interbrand
competition in the licensed products and that, in particular, this may
occur where the licensee's market share exceeds 40 per cent. See Article
10(9) for definition of "Licensee's market share" which includes licensed
products and other interchangeable products and services provided by
the licensee.

Below are set out the main provisions of the Technology Transfer
Block Exemption.

(ii) Fundamental aspects of Technology Transfer Block Exemption

Insert as new paragraph: The structure of the regulation broadly follows   **8.261B**
the PBE and KHBE. It applies to pure patent and know-how licences and
mixed patent/know-how licences. For the purposes of the regulation,
utility models, SPCs and plant breeders' rights are deemed to be patents.
Exclusive licences and, for limited periods, bans on active and passive
sales are exempted. Clauses that are generally not restrictive of competition are listed in Article 2 and these are specifically "white-listed" in case
they do restrict competition. Article 3 sets out the "black list" clauses
which, if contained in an agreement, will make it fall outside the block
exemption. Where a licence contains clauses which are restrictive of
competition but not covered in the regulation, then the agreements must
be notified to the Commission under the "opposition procedure" and if
the Commission does not oppose such exemption within four months
from the date of notification, the licence shall be deemed to fall within the
block exemption. As with the PBE and KHBE, the TTBE does not apply
to patent or know-how pools licences between competing undertakings
who hold interests in a joint venture and reciprocal licences between
competitors.[73a]

The TTBE comes into force on April 1, 1996 and remains in force for
10 years.

Add: FOOTNOTE 73a: Article 5.

(iii) *Exclusive licences and territorial restrictions — Article 1*

8.261C   Insert as new paragraph: Exclusive licences and bans on exploitation in other licensees' territories are exempted. Similarly, bans on active sales (*i.e.* advertising and establishment of commercial premises) and passive sales (*i.e.* responding to unsolicited orders from customers in other territories) in other licensees' or the licensor's territory are also exempted. However, exclusive licences and such bans are only permitted for certain periods of time and will depend on whether the licence is characterised as a pure patent licence, a pure know-how licence or a mixed licence.

(iv) *Period allowed for territorial protection under TTBE*

8.261D   Insert as new table and paragraph:

	Pure patent	**Pure know-how**	**Mixed**
Exclusive licence	As long as the licensed product is protected by parallel patents	10 years from date when licensed product first put on market within Community by one of licensees[4]	As long as the licensed product is protected by *necessary* patents otherwise same as pure know-how licence
Active sales ban	As long as the licensed product is protected by parallel patents	10 years from date when licensed product first put on market within Community by one of the licensees[4]	As long as the licensed product is protected by *necessary* patents otherwise same as pure know-how licence
Passive sales ban	5 years from date when licensed product first put on market within Community by one of the licensees	5 years from date when licensed product first put on market within Community by one of the licensees[4]	5 years from date when licensed product first put on market within Community by one of the licensees
Use of licensor's TM[1]	As long as the licensed product is protected by parallel patents	As long as know-how remains secret and substantial	Unspecified[3]
Use licence only[2]	As long as the licensed product is protected by parallel patents	As long as know-how remains secret and substantial	Unspecified[3]

[1]   An obligation on the licensee to use only the licensor's trademark or getup.

[2]   An obligation on the licensee to limit his production of the licensed product to the quantities he requires in manufacturing his own products and to sell the licensed product only as an integral part of or a replacement part for his own products.

³ Although unspecified, the common-sense approach is to take the longer of either the period for which the licensed product is protected by *necessary* patents or as long as the know-how remains secret and substantial. However, notification under Opposition Procedure is advisable.
⁴ Or until the know-how ceased to be secret and substantial (whichever is the shorter period).

Most agreements will be mixed patent/know-how licences. Accordingly, an important issue will be whether the patents are "necessary patents". The difference in permissible territorial protection could be 20 years. "Necessary patents" are defined as patents "where a licence under the patent is necessary for the putting into effect of the licensed technology in so far as, in the absence of such a licence, the realisation of the licensed technology would not be possible or would be possible only to a lesser extent or in more difficult or costly conditions. Such patents must therefore be of technical, legal or economic interests to the licensee."[73b] Difficulties could arise in proving that the patents are necessary and one is advised to read *Boussois v. Interpane* where a mixed patent/know-how licence was held not to fall within the PBE because the "patents were not necessary for achieving the objects of the licensed technology".[73c] Furthermore, difficulties may arise as to whether improvement patents are "necessary" to the exploitation of the licensed technology.
Add: FOOTNOTE 73b: Article 10(5).
Add: FOOTNOTE 73c: Para. 19 *et seq.*

(v) White-listed clauses

Insert as new paragraph: These are similar to the PBE and KHBE. Thus they include confidentiality clauses; bans on sublicences; post-term use bans; feed and grant back clauses; minimum quality specifications; legal assistance clauses: payment of royalties beyond the duration of the patents or know-how; field of use restrictions; minimum royalty; most favoured licensee; obligation to mark product with licensor's mark; not to construct facilities for third parties; obligation to supply only a particular customer as a second source; right to terminate licence if IP challenged; a right to terminate the licence if the licensee raises the claim that a patent is not necessary; best endeavour clause and a right to license others (*i.e.* terminated exclusivity) if licensee becomes involved in competing products. 8.261E

(vi) Black-listed clauses

Insert as new paragraph: The number of black-listed clauses has been reduced compared to the PBE and KHBE. The following are black-listed in the TTBE: 8.261F

(a) Price restriction clauses.

    (b) Non-competition clauses—a clause which prevents a party from carrying out R & D, production use or distribution of competing products is black-listed. However, a licensor can terminate the licence if the licensee becomes so involved.

    (c) Parallel import restraints.

    (d) Customer restraints where parties were competing manufacturers before grant of licence. The regulation is silent where the parties were not competing manufacturers and such clauses must be notified under the opposition procedure.

    (e) Quantity limits.

    (f) Obligation on licensee to assign back improvements.

    (g) Automatic prolongation of territorial protection by addition of new improvements.

(vii) Black-listed clauses under PBE, KHBE and TTBE

8.261G   Insert as new table:

Restraints	PBE	KHBE	TTBE
Strong feedback	Black-listed	Black-listed	Partially black-listed. No ban on exclusive licence of improvements to licensor
Tie-in/quality specifications	Black-listed	Black-listed	Must be notified under Opp. Proc.
No-challenge	Black-listed but right to terminate licence	Black-listed but right to terminate exclusivity of licence	Must be notified under Opp. Proc. if no right to terminate
Bans on dealing in competing products	Black-listed	Black-listed	Black-listed but if right to terminate it is white-listed
Customer restraints	Black-listed	Black-listed unless second source of supply	Black-listed only if parties already competing manufacturers otherwise notify under Opp. Proc. White-listed if licence intended to provide second source of supply
Quantity limits	Black-listed	Black-listed unless second source of supply or for integration into licensee's product	Black-listed unless second source of supply or for integration into licensee's product
Parallel import	Black-listed	Black-listed	Black-listed

Restraints	PBE	KHBE	TTBE
Price restrictions	Black-listed	Black-listed	Black-listed
Royalties (a) on products outside IP (b) after expiry of IP	(a) Black-listed (b) Black-listed unless to facilitate payment over period of time	(a) Black-listed (b) White-listed unless obligation continues where know-how became publicly known through licensor	(a) Not mentioned— notify under Opp. Proc. (b) White-listed unless obligation continues where know-how became publicly known through licensor
Automatic prolongation of licence	Black-listed unless right to terminate annually after expiry of initial term	Black-listed unless right to terminate every three years after initial term	Black-listed only if exclusivity rights prolonged beyond initial term

(viii) Opposition procedure

Insert as new paragraph: This is similar to that provided under the PBE   **8.261H**
and KHBE except the period of objection by the Commission is short-
ened to four months from the date of notification. In particular, quality
specifications/tie-ins and no-challenge clauses must be notified.

(ix) Withdrawal of exemption

Insert as new paragraph: The Commission may withdraw the benefit of   **8.261I**
the block exemption in four cases:

(a) There is no effective interbrand competition. The regulation
specifically states that may in particular occur where the licensee's market share exceeds 40 per cent. See Article 10(9) for
definition of "Licensee's market share" which includes licensed
products and other interchangeable products and services provided by the licensee.

(b) A licensee refuses to meet unsolicited demands from users in
other territories beyond the sanctioned period.

(c) Where parties hinder parallel trade.

(d) The parties were competing manufacturers at the date of grant
of the licence and obligations on the licensee to produce a
minimum quantity or to use his best endeavours have effectively
prevented the licensee from using competing technologies.

(x) Transitional provisions

Insert as new paragraph: The PBE initially was due to expire on Decem-   **8.261J**
ber 31, 1994 but this was extended twice until December 31, 1995. The

TTBE again retrospectively extends it to March 31, 1996. The KHBE was due to expire at the end of the century but has been prematurely repealed.

Agreements in force on March 31, 1996 which fulfil the exemption requirements laid down by the PBE or KHBE will continue to benefit from such exemption.

Chapter Nine

INTELLECTUAL PROPERTY AND JOINT VENTURES

2. Joint Ventures and Competition

Competition between parent companies — In *Re Agreements* 9.003
between British Telecommunications plc and MCI [1995] 5 C.M.L.R.
285, the Commission held that a joint venture between two major
telecommunications organisations fell within Article 85(1) because the
parent companies were potential competitors of the joint venture and of
each other in the market concerned and actual competitors in the overall
market of telecommunications.

CHAPTER TEN

FRANCHISING

4. COMMUNITY LAW AND FRANCHISE

(b) Exemption: Commission's decisions post-Pronuptia

10.013A   The Commission has issued a Green Paper on Vertical Restraints in E.C.
Competition Policy [1997] 4 C.M.L.R. 519 which is the result of a
detailed investigation into the competitive effects of vertical restraints in
distribution and franchising arrangements. It has proposed four options
—maintaining the current system; providing for wider block exemptions;
providing more focussed block exemptions and providing block exemptions with guidelines as compatibility of agreements with Article 85(1)
(*i.e.* for instance by providing a rebuttable presumption that a vertical
agreement between parties with less than 20 per cent market share is
compatible with Article 85(1)). The paper is not specifically aimed at
intellectual property licences but it is clear that such licences are also of
a vertical nature. For commentary, see *The E.C.'s Green Paper on Vertical Restraints: Franchising* John Adams [1998] E.I.P.R. 1

CHAPTER ELEVEN

ABUSE OF A DOMINANT POSITION

5. DOMINANT POSITION

(a) Relevant product or service market

See *Notice on the Definition of the Relevant Market for the Purposes of*   **11.006–**
Community Competition Law [1998] 4 C.M.L.R. 177 where the E.C.   **11.015**
Commission sets out in detail its approach to the determination of the
relevant product and geographic markets.

CHAPTER TWELVE

ENFORCEMENT OF E.C. AND EEA COMPETITION LAW

1. INTRODUCTION

12.001 With the principle of subsidiarity (recently reinforced by the Treaty of Amsterdam—see para 1.003) and the Commission's refusal to act on complaints regarding infringement of Articles 85 and 86 unless there was a Community interest, enforcement of Article 85 and 86 will fall increasingly on national competition authorities. The Commission has now issued a notice (*Notice on Cooperation between national competition authorities and the Commission in handling cases falling within the scope of Articles 85 and 86* [1997] 5 C.M.L.R. 884) which sets out the division of duties between the Commission and national competition authorities. Generally, both have concurrent jurisdiction to enforce Articles 85 and 86 but national competition authorities cannot grant exemption to an agreement (nor can it prohibit an exempted agreement). The notice provides that the Commission will usually handle cases where the businesses involved carry out the relevant activities in more than one Member State but that national competition authorities should enforce Articles 85 and 86 where such is not the case. Where a complaint to the Commission is rejected because of lack of Community interest, the Commission will ask the national competition authority to investigate and decide on the complaint.

3. COMPARISON OF ENFORCEMENT OF COMMUNITY LAW BY COMMISSION AND NATIONAL COURTS

12.004 FOOTNOTE 13. Add: In *Iberian U.K. Ltd v. B.P.B. Industries plc* [1996] 2 C.M.L.R. 601, High Court of England, Mr Justice Laddie held that national courts should take all reasonable steps to avoid or reduce the risk of arriving at a conclusion which is at variance with a decision of the Commission in relation to competition law. Furthermore, it would be contrary to public policy to allow persons who have been involved in competition proceedings in Europe to deny before national courts the correctness of the conclusions reached there.

4. NOTIFICATION OF AGREEMENTS TO COMMISSION

(b) Notification, negative clearance and exemption

12.011 Add to FOOTNOTE 33. In *Koninklijke Vereeniging ter Bevordering van de Belangen des Boekhandels v. Free Record Shop B.V. and or* [1997] 5

C.M.L.R. 521 (ECJ), the court following *Parfums Marcel Rochas* said that it is "settled case law" that agreements concluded after entry into force of Regulation 17 which are merely replicas of a standard contract concluded prior to its commencement and duly notified benefit from the same system of provisional validity as the standard notified contract. Advocate-General Lenz in his Opinion referred to *Delimitis* [1991] I E.C.R. 935; [1992] 5 C.M.L.R. 210 where the ECJ said at para 48 that the Court had consistently held that national courts may not where the Commission has given no decision under Regulation 17 declare automatically void under Article 85(2) agreements which were in existence prior to March 13, 1962 and have been duly notified. Thus, the law must be considered as granting provisional validity on "old" agreements provided they were notified prior to February 6, 1962. The issue of provisional validity for agreements which existed prior to that date but which were not notified still remains in doubt (see para 12.071 and FOOTNOTE 26).

If amendments are made to the standard form agreement which extend the restrictive nature of the standard terms agreement, then provisional validity will be removed unless the term is severable from the rest of the agreement in which case only the new restriction would not be covered by the provisional validity—*Koninklijke.*

5. NOTIFICATION FOR EXEMPTION OR NEGATIVE CLEARANCE: PROCEDURE AND PRACTICE

(b) Compulsory form for notification

The Antitrust Procedure (Applications and Notifications) Regulation 3385/94 can be found at [1995] 5 C.M.L.R. 507.   12.036

7. TERMINATION OF NOTIFICATION: PRACTICE AND PROCEDURE

(d) Adverse decision

End of first paragraph, add: In T–30/91, *Solvay SA v. E.C. Commission* 12.053 [1996] 5 C.M.L.R. 57, the CFI held that where inculpatory documents had not been disclosed to undertakings under investigation in Commission proceedings, the Commission must communicate such documents to those undertakings. Any adverse decision taken against such undertakings in the absence of such disclosure will result in the documents being excluded as evidence on appeal to CFI. Thus, a Commission's decision will only be annulled if the objection taken by the Commission could be proved only by reference to such documents. Even where such information is confidential, the right that undertakings have to protection of their business secrets must be balanced against the safeguarding of the rights of the defence—*Solvay.*

The Commission has issued a notice on the internal rules of procedure for processing requests for access to the file in cases pursuant to Articles 85 and 86—*Access to the File (Antitrust) Notice 1997* [1997] 4 C.M.L.R. 490. Generally, the Commission recognises the right of parties who are the subject of investigations to have full access to all documents which make up the file but also has regard to the protection of confidential information concerning firms. Thus, the Commission will take into account (i) the relevance of the information to determining whether an infringement has been committed (ii) its probative value (iii) whether it is indispensable (iv) the degree of sensitivity involved (v) the seriousness of the infringement. Each document will be assessed to determine whether the need to disclose it is greater than the harm which might result from disclosure.

It should be noted that a complainant does not have the same rights to access a file as an alleged infringer. Nevertheless, a complainant may request access to the documents on which the Commission has based its position but cannot have access to confidential information belonging to the firms complained of or to third party firms.

9. COMPLAINTS

12.055 FOOTNOTE 48: Add: In considering the Community interest, there is a balance between the significance of the alleged infringement and the extent of the investigative measures required for the Commission to perform under the best possible conditions its task of making sure that Articles 85 and 86 are complied with. If the alleged anti-competitive effects are confined to the territory of a Member State and there are proceedings before the national competition authority, the Commission can reject the complaint for a lack of Community interest—see *BEMIM v. E.C. Commission* [1996] 4 C.M.L.R. 305. See also para 12.001.

See also T–77/92, *Parker Pen Limited v. E.C. Commission* [1995] 5 C.M.L.R. 435 where interestingly, Parker Pen submitted that the Commission had no interest in bringing proceedings against it, *i.e.* there was no Community interest. The CFI rejected the argument by referring to the Commission's finding that the export ban complained of was capable of affecting trade between Member States to an appreciable extent. This finding is interesting because it equates Community interest with the jurisdiction of Article 85(1)—if a wrongful act falls within Article 85(1), *i.e.* affects trade between Member States, then there is a Community interest. Furthermore, it is interesting because it was certainly not clear that the absence of Community interest meant that the Commission could not act. Rather, it could be said that it was a self-imposed rule that the Commission was not obliged to act in such circumstances. The Commission has issued a notice that only where businesses carry out the relevant activities in more than one Member State will there be a Community interest—see para 12.001.

End of third paragraph, add: The Commission is entitled to reject a complaint under Article 3 without giving a formal decision but must examine carefully the facts and law before refusing to initiate proceedings—*Koelman v. E.C. Commission* [1996] 4 C.M.L.R. 636.

Recently, there have been two authorities on the issue of direct and individual concern where a complaint has been made about a decision by E.C. Commission to grant exemption to a selective distribution network. In *Case 87/92 BVBA Kruidvat v. EC Commission* [1998] ETMR 395; [1997] 3 C.M.L.R. 1046, Kruidvat sought annulment of a Commission decision whereby it granted Parfums Givenchy S.A. individual exemption to its selective distribution network. Kruidvat was not a member of the selective distribution network but had sold GIVENCHY products which it procured on the parallel market. Kruidvat had not been involved in the process granting exemption so it could not claim that the decision was not addressed to it nor had Kruidvat ever applied to join the network. Moreover, the Court held that its action was inadmissible under Article 173 because the decision did not distinguish Kruidvat from other economic operators within the parallel market.

12.060

However, in Case T–19/92 *Groupement D'Achat Edouard Leclerc v. E.C. Commission* [1997] 4 C.M.L.R. 995 (Court of First Instance), it was held that an operator who has been refused admission to a selective distribution network and who has submitted observations pursuant to Article 19(3) of Regulation 17 is directly and individually concerned by a Commission decision adopting a favourable position pursuant to Article 19(3) of Regulation 17 towards the selection criteria (following the decision in Case 75/84 *Metro v E.C. Commission* [1986] E.C.R. 3021; [1987] 1 C.M.L.R. 118).

On the strength of the above decision, it is unlikely that an application to join the network *after* a decision to grant individual exemption has been made would confer *locus standi* on the applicant to challenge the Commission's decision. Thus, one must conclude that there is an element of timing involved moreover, the complainant must apply to join the network.

12. NATIONAL COURTS AND ARTICLES 85 AND 86

(b) Concurrent proceedings in national court and before the Commission

See *Iberian U.K. Ltd v. B.P.B. Industries plc* [1996] 2 C.M.L.R. 601, High Court of England where Mr Justice Laddie held that it would be contrary to public policy to allow persons who have been involved in competition proceedings in Europe to deny before national courts the correctness of the conclusions reached there. See also para. 12.004.

12.067

Footnote 11, add "This decision was appealed. See para 12.070".

12.069

12–070   In *MTV Europe v. B.M.G. Record Limited* [1995] 1 C.M.L.R 437, the Plaintiff complained in June 1992 to the E.C. Commission that the defendant was in breach of Articles 85 and 86. In May 1993, the Commission issued a preliminary assessment in favour of the Plaintiff. In August 1993, the Plaintiff brought proceedings claiming damages for breach of Articles 85 and 86 in the English courts. In September 1993, the defendants notified their agreements (of which complaint had been made) to the Commission seeking negative clearance and/or exemption under Article 85(3). In March 1994, the Commission stated that on the information then available it considered that there were grounds for finding that the arrangements did infringe Article 85(1) and did not satisfy the conditions for exemption under Article 85(3). Shortly thereafter, an application for a stay of the UK proceedings pending the outcome of the Commission proceedings was heard in the High Court. At first instance, the judge took a commonsense view and held that it would not be right to form a concluded view as to the likely outcome of the Commission proceedings and that it would not be right to proceed to judgment prior to that decision. Instead of granting a general stay, he permitted the case to continue in the light of an undertaking from the Plaintiff that it would not set the matter down for trial until 1 month after the Commission had issued its decision.

On appeal *MTV v. B.M.G.* [1997] 1 C.M.L.R. 867, the Court of Appeal held that despite arguments to the contrary law, the judge did have jurisdiction in cases where the outcome was not clear to permit the preparation of proceedings to go ahead until a point short of decision. Furthermore, the Court of Appeal held that the potential injustice of prolonged delay could outweigh the potential prejudice to the defendant of having to be involved in two separate proceedings which could be compensated in costs. The Court of Appeal reaffirmed the basic approach set out in para 12.070

Footnote 13 , Add "[1994] I E.C.R. 5641; [1996] 4 C.M.L.R. 191" as reference for case *Gottrup-Klin and ors v. Dansk Landbrugs.*

(d) Practice and procedure in English courts where Article 85 or 86 is in issue

(iv) Stay of proceedings

12.090   The approach by the judge in *MTV Europe v B.M.G. and ors* was upheld by the Court of Appeal (see *MTV Europe v. B.M.G. and ors* [1997] 1 C.M.L.R. 867 and discussion at para 12.070 above).

See *Iberian U.K. Ltd v. BPB Industries plc* [1996] 2 C.M.L.R. 601, High Court of England where Mr Justice Laddie states that national courts should take all reasonable steps to avoid the risk of arriving at a conclusion which is at variance with the Commission in relation to competition law and except in the clearest cases of breach or non-breach, it should stay proceedings before a national court to await the outcome of proceedings before the Commission or European Courts.

Note also that where such a process has taken place, the parties will not be permitted to re-litigate the same issues in subsequent national proceedings—*Iberian ibid.* and discussed at paras 12.067 and 12.004.

The Court of Justice has given guidance to national courts in relation to **12.093** references under Article 177—*Guidance on references by national courts for preliminary rulings* [1997] 1 C.M.L.R. 78. This can be summarised as follows:

(a) Courts or tribunals against whose decisions there is no judicial remedy under national law must refer questions of interpretation arising before them unless the Court has already ruled on the point or unless the correct application of the rule of Community law is obvious

(b) Where a national court intends to question the validity of a Community act, it must refer that question to the Court of Justice but may reject a plead challenging the validity of such an act (see also recent case of *Woodspring District Council v. Bakers of Nailsea* C–27/95 [1997] 2 C.M.L.R. 265)

(c) Where the national court has serious doubts about the validity of a Community act, it may grant interim or suspensory relief

(d) The order for reference should contain a statement of reasons which is succinct but sufficiently complete to give the Court, and those to whom it must be notified, a clear understanding of the factual and legal context of the proceedings. In particular, it should include

  (i) a statement of the facts which are essential to a full understanding of the legal significance of the main proceedings

  (ii) an exposition of the national law which may be applicable

  (iii) a statement of the reasons which have prompted the national court to refer the question or questions to the Court of Justice and

  (iv) where appropriate, a summary of the arguments of the parties.

It is desirable that a decision to refer should not be taken until the national court is able to define, if only as a working hypothesis, the factual and legal context of the question; such is best done after both sides have been heard.

CHAPTER THIRTEEN

JURISDICTION AND INTELLECTUAL PROPERTY

1. INTRODUCTION

13.001A Insert as new paragraph: In a study by Adams set out in his article "Choice of Forum in Patent Disputes" [1995] EIPR 497, he compares different aspects of patent litigation in England and Wales, Scotland, France and Germany. The following points can be made:

Interlocutory relief: Generally good in all jurisdictions apart from France. In England and Wales, matters are complicated because of the need to show that damages are not an adequate remedy.

Cross-examination of parties: This is commonplace in the United Kingdom but not in France and Germany.

Construction of claims: Traditionally narrow in England and Wales and Scotland, broader in France and broader still in Germany.

Discovery of documents: Automatic in England and Wales (although recent judge-led steps have been taken to restrict discovery in appropriate cases); in Scotland, discovery is available on application. In France and Germany, the courts can order a party to produce a document but it is nothing like the United Kingdom discovery process.

2. BRUSSELS CONVENTION

13.002A The Brussels Convention must be interpreted autonomously and without reference to Member States' own jurisdictional rules—Case C–383/95 *Rutten v. Cross Medical* [1997] All E.R. (E.C.) 121. See also Case 97/1367 *Julio Cesar Palmaz and ors v. Boston Scientific B.V. and ors* and Case No. 97/1368 *Expandable Grafts Partnership and ors v. Boston Scientific B.V. and ors* [1998] F.S.R. 199 (English translation of Dutch judgment delivered October 29, 1997) at 212 where the District Court of The Hague stated that Articles 16 and 19 of the Brussels or Lugano Convention must be interpreted autonomously in accordance with the conventions.

13.003 In *Gareth Pearce v. Ove Arup Partnership Limited and ors* [1997] F.S.R. 641, an English plaintiff sued an English defendant in England for breach of Dutch copyright. The Defendant argued that the *Moçambique* and double actionability rules were respectively an English choice of law rule and a justiciability rule, neither of which was concerned with jurisdiction (see para 13.044). The English High Court rejected these arguments and held that the Brussels Convention overrode both rules.

This case was followed in *Coin Controls Limited v. Suzo International (UK) Limited* [1997] F.S.R. 660, where the Court held that the Brussels Convention can force the courts of a Contracting State to entertain foreign infringement proceedings in the Member State where the defendant is domiciled. Furthermore, it held that domestic rules such as the rule in *Moçambique* cannot be used to circumvent Article 2.

Both these decisions mean that one can bring proceedings in a Contracting State in respect of an infringement either in the domicile of the defendant or the state where the infringement took place *i.e.* the fundamental rules of the Brussels Convention apply to infringement proceedings. This judgment was approved by the Court of Appeal in *Fort Dodge Limited v. Akzo Nobel N.V.* [1998] F.S.R. 222 at 242. Moreover, the Court of Appeal held that such a conclusion was not contrary to the Paris Convention of 1883 or the Agreement of Trade-Related Aspects of Intellectual Property Rights (TRIPS).

See further 13.013.

(c) Derogations from the defendant's "domicile" rule

(ii) Exclusive jurisdiction

Article 17

In *Kitechnology BV v. Unicor GmbH Plastmaschinen* [1995] F.S.R. 765   **13.008** (English Court of Appeal), the Court was concerned with express jurisdiction clauses which conferred jurisdiction on the English court and which were contained in confidentiality agreements which were signed by a person interested in acquiring a right to manufacture the other party's pipes. The Court held that the clauses covered not only claims for breach of contract but also claims for misuse of confidential information closely connected with them.

(d) Intellectual property and Brussels Convention

(i) Infringement action—Article 5(3)

At end of second paragraph, add: In *Kitechnology v. Unicor*, above, the   **13.010** English Court of Appeal held that a claim for breach of confidence did not arise in tort and was non-contractual. However, it noted that there had been a reference to the ECJ in *Barclays Bank plc v. Glasgow City Council* [1994] Q.B. 404 [1994] 2 W.L.R. 466 as to whether a restitutionary claim fell within the phrase "matters relating to tort, delict or quasi-delict" and that an equitable claim for breach of confidence was indistinguishable in principle and thus the Court considered the matter *sub judice.*

However, the Court said that it was settled law following *Bier BV v. Mines de Potasse* and *Dumez France and Tracoba v. Hessiche Landesbank* [1990] 1 E.C.R. 49 that the place where the harmful event occurred could either be the place where some damage was sustained or the place where the event which gave rise to and was the origin of such damage took place. However, following *Dumez,* it was necessary to distinguish between damage directly and indirectly caused. Indirect damage is not within Article 5(3) and thus precludes consideration of the place where financial loss resulting from the damage complained of is sustained by the injured plaintiff.

The Court then went on to consider whether the plaintiff had suffered damage in the U.K. It held that the plaintiff had not shown that there had been a harmful event in England in the sense of damage directly caused to them by the defendant's activities in Germany. It suggested that such damage might have been caused by, for instance, importation of pipes or machinery into this country from Germany which had been produced in breach of confidence in Germany. It rejected a submission that the value of the plaintiffs' rights as licensor had been damaged as this would enable them to establish jurisdiction in any country regardless of whether or not the defendant's activities had any effect upon their commercial interest there. The Court said that this would be a major derogation from the general rule stated in Article 2.

Accordingly, in an infringement action, if a plaintiff wishes to establish jurisdiction outside the country where the actual act that gave rise to infringement occurred, he must show some real tangible damage in another jurisdiction which is independent of the fact that his business is situated in that jurisdiction.

In *Mecklermedia Corp v. D.C. Congress Gesellschaft mbH* [1997] F.S.R. 627, the Plaintiffs brought an action in passing off. The Plaintiffs had used extensively the name "Internet World" in England in relation to the organisation of trade shows and the publishing of a magazine under the same name in England. The defendants were in the same business and had also organised a trade fair called "Internet World" in Germany. Indeed, they were the owner of a registered trade mark for "Internet World" in Germany. There had been a number of proceedings brought. In the instant case, the Plaintiff brought an action in England for passing off in England claiming that the use of "Internet World" in Germany by the Defendant gave rise to confusion and was damaging to the goodwill in the United Kingdom (the constituents of passing off are reputation, deception and damage). The Defendant submitted that Article 5(3) did not confer jurisdiction on English courts. The judge disagreed stating that to do acts abroad which led to damage of goodwill within the UK by misleading the public in Germany was passing off. England was the place of the harmful event as under the law of passing off, the harm was to the goodwill in England.

In *Coin Controls Limited v. Suzo International (U.K.) Limited* [1997] F.S.R. 660, the Court held that the Brussels Convention can force the courts of a Contracting State to entertain foreign infringement proceedings.

(1) Extraterritorial pan-European injunctions

At end of second paragraph, add: In *Plastus Kreativ AB v. Minnesota Mining* now reported at [1995] R.P.C. 438, the plaintiff sought a declaration that its activities in France, Germany and the United Kingdom did not constitute an infringement of the defendant's European patent granted in those countries. Mr Justice Aldous struck out the parts of the pleading referring to infringement in Germany and France because he held that there had been no claim by the defendants that the plaintiff had so infringed such patents and, accordingly, the case law meant that the plaintiff was not entitled to such a declaration. However, he went on to consider a submission from the counsel for the defendants that the pleading should be struck out because patents were strictly territorial in nature and were governed by local law and were only justiciable in the country in which the patent was granted. Mr Justice Aldous commented that there were good policy grounds for having an infringement matter decided in the state in where it arises (at 447).   **13.011**

It is submitted that whilst there may be good policy grounds, that does not permit derogation from the Brussels Convention. Thus if the action is brought against the Defendant in the state of his domicile, then an injunction restraining the Defendant from infringing in those countries where the Plaintiff owns parallel rights would be permissible. In this case, the defendant was an American company so *prima facie* the Brussels Convention did not apply. Mr Justice Aldous' statements go more to the issue of *forum conveniens* which is specifically held to be inapplicable where it is inconsistent with the Brussels Convention (see para 13.046).

In Case 97/1367 *Julio Cesar Palmaz and ors v Boston Scientific B.V. and ors* and Case No. 97/1368 *Expandable Grafts Partnership and ors v. Boston Scientific B.V. and ors* [1998] F.S.R. 199 (English translation of Dutch judgment delivered 29.10.1997), the District Court of the Hague followed *Lincoln/Interglas* in upholding the right of Dutch court to have jurisdiction to award injunctions restraining infringement of foreign patents against a person who is party to Dutch proceedings.

In *Coin Controls Limited v. Suzo International (U.K.) Limited* [1997] F.S.R. 660, Mr Justice Laddie held that where United Kingdom and foreign patents are identical (or not materially different), the proceedings can be regarded as related for the purposes of Article 6(1). He said that they may be materially different where the patents were applied for   **13.013** separately through the national patent offices or because they began life as an EPC application but have been subject to different amendments in different countries after grant. However, in *Fort Dodge Limited v. Akzo Nobel N.V.* [1998] F.S.R. 222 (English Court of Appeal), the Court said, in considering *Kalfelis* and the risk of irreconcilable judgments, that there is no risk of irreconcilable judgments in relation to parallel patents because a judgment on infringement in the UK will depend upon a national right having effect only in the UK and similarly for a judgment in Holland on a Dutch patent. Thus, whilst there may be much to commend hearing parallel infringement proceedings together, it could not be said that there was a risk of irreconcilable judgments. However, they did not consider the matter *acte claire* and thus this has been referred to the European Court of Justice.

In the Netherlands, in *Case No. 97/1296 Expandable Grafts, Ethicon and Cordis v. Boston Scientific and others,*—April 23, 1998 unreported, [overturning the decision in Case 97/1367 *Julio Cesar Palmaz and ors v. Boston Scientific B.V. and ors* and Case No. 97/1368 *Expandable Grafts Partnership and ors v. Boston Scientific BV and ors* [1998] F.S.R. 199 (English translation of Dutch judgment delivered October 29, 1997) where it was held that a Dutch court has *per se* jurisdiction under Article 6(1) over infringers of parallel patents where one or more defendants are Dutch], the Court of Appeal for the Netherlands held that Article 6(1) is a special jurisdictional rule which should be interpreted narrowly because defendants should normally be sued in their country of domicile. It said that the object of Article 6 is to avoid irreconcilable judgments but that the possibility of different judgments is inherent in the European patents and such judgments were not irreconcilable. However, the court said that where several companies belonging to one group of companies are selling identical products in different national markets, this should be considered as one joint action based on a joint business plan leading to simultaneous hearing and settlement of cases under Article 6(1). However, it said that such actions may only be brought in the domicile of the state where the head office is. It is submitted that this last observation although one of common sense is an unacceptable gloss on the plain wording of Article 6(1). If there is no risk of irreconcilable judgments, then they are not related and consolidation of actions under Article 6(1) is not permissible.

N.B. Article 6(1) will only apply if the Defendant is domiciled in a Contracting State. Thus, where an English company which is the holder of a European Patent which is protected in England, France and Italy sues for patent infringement in all three countries respectively an English, French and Italian company for acts carried out in those countries, it may be that the court first seized could try all actions. Thus, if it was an English court first seized, the English court could try all actions. However, if it was an American company carrying out the acts complained of in Italy, the English court cannot claim jurisdiction over the Italian proceedings and thus the Italian proceedings could not be consolidated with the French and English proceedings in England.

In *Fort Dodge Limited v. Akzo Nobel N.V.* [1998] F.S.R. 222 (English **13.015** Court of Appeal), the Court of Appeal has said without discussion of any authorities, that the measures referred to in Article 24 must be granted "in aid of or as an adjunct to some final determination then in contemplation".

In *Case No. 97/1296 Expandable Grafts, Ethicon and Cordis v. Boston* **13.022** *Scientific and others,*—April 23, 1998 unreported, the Court of Appeal for the Netherlands held that Article 24 only permits a court to impose interim measures in the territory of the state of the court. Thus, the Court held that injunctions under Article 24 against foreign defendants in respect of their actions in another Member State should not be imposed.

In *Fort Dodge Limited v. Akzo Nobel N.V.* [1998] F.S.R. 222 (English Court of Appeal), the English Court of Appeal considered the issue as to whether a Dutch court could grant an interim order restraining defendants from carrying out acts in England which they alleged infringed its parallel English patent. The Court held that where English courts have exclusive jurisdiction over a dispute concerning an English patent because the Defendant had put in issue the validity of the patent, it would be vexatious for a Dutch court to grant an interim order seeking to restrain alleged acts of infringement in England (at 245). However, as they did not consider that it was *acte claire* that in infringement proceedings of a foreign patent where validity of the patent is put in issue that meant that the court seized of the infringement proceedings must decline jurisdiction, they referred the matter to the ECJ under Article 177.

The finding by the English Court of Appeal that it would be vexatious for a court of a Contracting State to make an extraterritorial interim order if it had no jurisdiction over substantive issue is important. For instance, a distinction should be made in considering the ability of a court to grant an extraterritorial interim order between courts seized under Article 2 (*i.e.* the court of the defendant's domicile) and Article 5(3) (the state where the infringement took place). Under Article 2, the court will have jurisdiction in the substantive matter in relation to all acts of intellectual property infringement carried out in any Contracting State by the Defendant. Where a court's jurisdiction is based solely on Article 5(3), its jurisdiction in the substantive matter is limited to those acts carried out in the Contracting State of that court. By parity of reasoning set out in the *Fort Dodge* case, arguments that a court should have the power to grant extraterritorial interim orders will be more likely to succeed in the former case because the court will have substantive final extraterritorial jurisdiction whereas in the latter, it will not (assuming no attack on validity).

In the context of Article 22, the court held in *Mecklermedia Corp v. D.C.* **13.023** *Congress Gesellschaft mbH* [1997] F.S.R. 627, that a licensee cannot be regarded as the same party as the licensor (cf *Berkeley Administration v. McClelland* [1995] I.L.Pr 201 where the English Court of Appeal said that in the context of Article 21, it was "wholly unreal" to separate a wholly owned subsidiary from its parent.)

In Case 97/1367 *Julio Cesar Palmaz and ors v. Boston Scientific B.V. and ors* and Case No. 97/1368 *Expandable Grafts Partnership and ors v. Boston Scientific BV and ors* [1998] F.S.R. 199 (English translation of Dutch judgment delivered October 29, 1997), the District Court of The Hague held that Article 21 does not apply in the case of interim measures in proceedings for infringement of parallel national patents because it is "out of the question" that an interim measure could be considered contrary to a decision in a procedure on the merits.

13.025 In *Mecklermedia Corp v. D.C. Congress Gesellschaft mbH* [1997] F.S.R 627, there were three sets of proceedings. In Germany, the Defendant had brought proceedings against the Plaintiff's licensee for using its registered mark "Internet World". As a result, the Plaintiff had brought their own proceedings in Germany against the Defendant from using the name "Internet World" and for cancellation of the German marks. Subsequently, the Plaintiff brought proceedings in England to restrain the Defendant from passing off in England. The judge held they were not related proceedings for the purposes of Article 23 because there was no risk of irreconcilable judgments.

Under Article 6(1), the issue of relatedness is similar to that under Article 22, namely whether there is a risk of irreconcilable judgments. Thus, the decisions under that Article are relevant to Article 23 — see para 13.013. In *Coin Controls Limited v. Suzo International (U.K.) Limited* [1997] F.S.R 660, the Court held that patent infringement proceedings based on parallel patents were related for the purpose of Article 6(1). However, in *Fort Dodge Limited v. Akzo Nobel NV* [1998] F.S.R. 222, the English Court of Appeal held in considering Article 6(1) that proceedings based on infringement of parallel patents did not give rise to a risk of irreconcilable judgments. However, it did not consider it *acte claire* and has referred the matter to the E.C.J.

In Case 97/1367 *Julio Cesar Palmaz and ors v. Boston Scientific B.V. and ors* and Case No. 97/1368 *Expandable Grafts Partnership and ors v. Boston Scientific B.V. and ors* [1998] F.S.R. 199 (English translation of Dutch judgment delivered October 29, 1997), the District Court of The Hague, having held that Article 22 did give it jurisdiction to stay proceedings brought in Dutch courts since interim measures may be closely connected with proceedings instituted earlier elsewhere said that it was inappropriate because such would not be expedient in view of decent legal protection of the proprietor of the patent. The court said to stay proceedings in favour of the first seized court would favour a "race to the court".

Thus, the position as to whether Article 22 *prima facie* applies to parallel patent infringement proceedings and if it does, how the discretion should be exercised is unclear. One awaits a ruling from the ECJ on this point. The main problems are (a) Do parallel proceedings give rise to a danger of irreconcilable judgments (b) How should a court exercise its discretion where there are several proceedings involving parallel rights.

(v) Proceedings concerned with registration of validity of intellectual property rights

(2) Unregistered rights

See Jooris, "Infringement of Foreign Copyright and The Jurisdiction of   **13.029**
English Courts" [1996] 3 EIPR 139 where he discusses whether copyright is immoveable and where he appears to conclude that copyright is immoveable. He also submits that an action concerning infringement of copyright cannot be considered to fall within Article 16(1), *i.e.* English court will not have jurisdiction in the case of a foreign infringement of an English copyright (although it is difficult to see in what circumstances acts abroad will infringe copyright bestowed under English law).

In England, it has been decided at first instance that intellectual property is not immoveable property. See para 13.044 below.

There have been a number of cases, English and Dutch, about what a   **13.030**
court should do when it has a case involving infringement of a foreign patent where validity is put in issue. The English courts favour declining jurisdiction over the whole case whereas the Dutch courts favour staying the infringement proceedings pending determination of the validity proceedings in the Contracting State where the patent is registered. These cases are now looked at in detail.

In *Coin Controls Limited v. Suzo International (U.K.) Limited* [1997] F.S.R. 660, the Plaintiff brought an action for infringement of foreign patents in the United Kingdom. The court held that as the validity of the patents were in issue, the whole action including infringement must be determined in the countries where the patents are registered. This course of action represents none of the three options proposed in the book. It however does commend itself by reason of simplicity. The court held that there was some attraction to deciding the issue of infringement but not validity but held that the two were inseparable because one cannot infringe an invalid claim. This approach was upheld in *Fort Dodge Limited v. Akzo Nobel N.V.* [1998] F.S.R. 222 (English Court of Appeal) where the Court held often one cannot form a view on infringement without considering the validity of the patent. Firstly, one cannot infringe an invalid patent. Secondly, there is the *Gillette* "squeeze" defence where it is alleged that the patent is invalid if the alleged infringing acts fall within the ambit of the claims. Thirdly, attacks on invalidity in infringement proceedings often provoke applications to amend the patent which would have effect from the date of grant of the patent so that it impinges on the issue of infringement.

In Case 97/1367 *Julio Cesar Palmaz and ors v. Boston Scientific BV and ors* and Case No. 97/1368 *Expandable Grafts Partnership and ors v. Boston Scientific B.V. and ors* [1998] F.S.R. 199 (English translation of Dutch judgment delivered October 29, 1997), the District Court of the Hague held that a Dutch court should *stay* proceedings for infringement pending the determination of the validity in the country of registration. Its judgment followed the reasoning in *Coin Controls* but rejected its conclusion to decline jurisdiction. Its reasons that a stay was appropriate were (a) Article 16(4) should be interpreted restrictively (b) pleas of invalidity could be solely to remove jurisdiction from the court first seizes (c) there is no good reason why infringement should be decided in the country of registration (d) the English interpretation would mean that jurisdiction would not be established until after the defence has been pleaded which would be contrary to the Brussels and/or Lugano Convention and should thus only be chosen if such was unavoidable which it was not (the Court relied on the fact that in Germany infringement and validity are tried by different courts and such has proven workable).

This case has been appealed. In Case No. 97/1296 *Expandable Grafts, Ethicon and Cordis v. Boston Scientific and others,*—April 23, 1998 unreported, the Court of Appeal for the Netherlands held that infringement and nullity are indissolubly linked to each other. It however upheld the finding that proceedings should be stayed until the foreign court has pronounced judgment on the nullity issue.

13.041 FOOTNOTE 67, Add "Applied in *Mecklermedia Corp v. D.C. Congress Gesellschaft mbH* [1997] F.S.R. 627.

(g) Intellectual property, English law and Brussels Convention

(i) Immoveable v. moveable distinction

13.044 As to whether copyright is immoveable or moveable, see Jooris, *ibid.*

In *Gareth Pearce v. Ove Arup Partnership Limited and ors* [1997] F.S.R. 641, an English plaintiff sued an English defendant in England for breach of Dutch copyright. The High Court held that the Brussels Convention overrode the *Moçambique* rule and the double actionability rule. In doing so, the court rejected an argument that these rules were a choice of law rule and a justiciability rule, neither of which was concerned with jurisdiction.

Add at end; In *Gareth Pearce v. Ove Arup Partnership Limited and ors*, the court held that it was difficult to regard copyright as immoveable property under English conflict of laws rules. The judge noted the *Potter v. Broken Hill* decision but said that it did not follow that it is to be classified as immoveable for all conflict of laws purposes. He noted that Dicey & Morris considered intangibles as moveables even though they cannot be moved. In the end, the judge did not decide the point. However, in *Coin Controls Limited v. Suzo International (U.K.) Limited* [1997] F.S.R 660, the High Court held that patents and other intellectual property rights are not accurately described as immoveables.

In *Coin Controls Limited v. Suzo International (U.K.) Limited* [1997] F.S.R 660, the Court held that the rule in *Moçambique* had not been abolished by s.10(a) Private Law (Miscellaneous Provisions) Act which abolishes the double actionability rule as the *Moçambique* rule had nothing to do with the double actionability rule but was based on public policy (N.B. There appears to be an obvious error in the report wherein it refers to the Civil Evidence Act 1995 rather than the Private law (Miscellaneous Provisions) Act 1995).

See *Gareth Pearce v. Ove Arup Partnership Limited and ors* and *Coin Controls Limited v. Suzo International (U.K.) Limited* where the issue as to whether copyright and patents were immoveable was discussed (see para 13.044).   **13.045**

(iii) Forum non conveniens

In a case where a plaintiff brought an action against a defendant in England and New York, the English court granted an injunction restraining the plaintiff from bringing an action based on the same facts and subject matter as the English proceedings against the defendant in New York on the basis that the forum conveniens was England and that substantial injustice that would be caused to the defendant by permitting the plaintiff to sue him in both jurisdictions—*Advanced Portfolio Technologies Inc. v. Ainsworth* [1996] F.S.R. 217 (High Court of England).   **13.046**

N.B. The "double actionability" rule has now been abolished—see 13.051 below.

In *Gareth Pearce v. Ove Arup Partnership Limited and ors* (above), the High Court held that the double actionability rule was a rule which although not a rule as to jurisdiction, was of equivalent effect and inconsistent with the mandatory nature of the Brussels Convention and its basic rules as to domicile-based jurisdiction (at p.654). Followed in *Coin Controls Limited v. Suzo International (U.K.) Limited* where the Court rejected an argument that a distinction should be drawn between jurisdiction over particular defendants and jurisdiction over subject matter which is more precisely referred to as justiciability.   **13.050**

(vii) The Private International Law (Miscellaneous Provisions) Bill

The Private International Law (Miscellaneous Provisions) Act came into force on May 1, 1996 (S.I. 1996 No. 995).   **13.051**

In Case 97/1367 *Julio Cesar Palmaz and ors v. Boston Scientific B.V. and ors* and Case No. 97/1368 *Expandable Grafts Partnership and ors v. Boston Scientific B.V. and ors* [1998] F.S.R. 199 (English translation of   **13.056**

Dutch judgment delivered October 29, 1997), the District Court dismissed an argument that Article 57 of the Brussels and Lugano Convention when interpreted in conjunction with Article 64(3) of the European Patent Convention (that lays down that infringements of European patents are to be examined in conformity with national law) meant that national procedural laws apply to the exclusion of the Brussels and Lugano Convention (*impliciter* an English court can only try an English patent). Although not cited, a finding to the contrary would have been in conflict with the Jenard report that proceedings for infringement of patents are governed by the "general rules of the Convention".

INDEX

(All references are to paragraph numbers)